GROUPS, TEAMS AND GROUPWORK REVISITED

GROUPS, TEAMS AND GROUPWORK REVISITED

A Theory, Methodology and Practice for the 21st Century

Seán Gaffney, Ph.D.

Foreword by
Marie-Anne Chidiac, D. Psych.

©2013, Ravenwood Press

No part of this publication may be reproduced, stored in a retrieval system or transmitted in any form or by any means electronic, mechanical or otherwise without the prior written permission of the publisher.

Copyrighted materials included in this work are reproduced under the provisions of the Copyright Act (1968) and the Copyright Amendment Act (1989).

Developed and Published by the
Ravenwood Press a subsidiary of the
Illawarra Gestalt Centre.
P.O. Box 141 Peregian Beach
Queensland
AUSTRALIA.

Cover illustration, text design and art work: B O'Neill
Made and printed in Australia by University of Wollongong Printers

ISBN

For more information on Ravenwood Press
Email: boneill@uow.edu.au
Website: www.illawarragestalt.org
 Or write to

Brian O'Neill
Illawarra Gestalt Centre
P.O. Box 141 Peregian Beach Queensland AUSTRALIA.

Dedication

Edwin C. Nevis
Teacher, Mentor, Colleague, Friend, Buddy

For always leading by example,
warts and all.

Acknowledgements

To Anne Maclean, Christchurch, New Zealand, my "First Reader": as always Anne, you generously followed and commented on the various drafts of this work.

To all the members of The Belfast Supervision and Training Group, 1996 onwards and ongoing, for your collegial contributions to my evolution as a Gestalt practitioner-theorist.

To all the members of the Peer Group in England – individually and collectively, we have been grists for each others' mills!

Contents

Foreword by Marie-Anne Chidiac   page xi

PART 1
1) Opening Statement of Intent   page xvii

2) Explanatory Reader Notes   page xxi

3) Who I am and what I do   page xxiii

4) Introduction   page 31

5) Philosophical Considerations   page 39

5) Field Perspectives   page 55

7) Cross-Cultural Perspectives   page 71

PART 2
8) Introductory Guidelines and Terminology   page 91

9) Social Groups, Work Groups and Teams   page 97

10) Social Groups, Work-Groups and Teams: Part 2   page 111

11) Another Trio of Groups in the Room   page 129

PART 3

12) A Focus on the   page 147
Practice of Groupwork

13) Applying this Approach   page 177
in an Organisational Setting

Vignettes

Vignette 1, Singapore   *page 49*

Vignette 2, Sweden   *page 65*

Vignette 3, Multicultural/   *page 76*
South West African

Vignette 4, Multicultural/Latin   *page 77*

Vignette 5, Multicultural   *page 77*

Vignette 6, Sweden   *page 97*

Vignette 7, Ghana   *page 114*

Vignette 8, Sweden   *page 123*

Vignette 9, Sweden   *page 125*

Vignette 10, Sweden   *page 133*

Vignette 11, Denmark   *page 136*

Vignette 12, Australia   *page 177*

Foreword
by
Marie-Anne Chidiac, D.Psych.

Foreword

Working in or with a group is now the norm for leaders, managers, coaches, Organisational Development (OD) practitioners or community organisers. Teams and work groups are today viewed as organisational building blocks with the focus of OD interventions shifting towards improving the performance of teams rather than individuals - as can be witnessed in the more recent growth of team coaching. The myth of the leader as the "lone hero" has collapsed as team virtues of co-operation and increased relationality are emphasised and often linked with improved performance, better outcomes and results.

As well as this renewed interest in working with groups and teams, the expansion of organisations into global markets is setting increasing challenges to forming culturally diverse teams. Companies must address team dynamics to meet performance goals with team members who are physically dispersed as well as culturally diverse. It is exactly this type of complexity and embedded-ness of groups and teams in their social and functional roles that Gaffney addresses in this book.

New methodologies are best based on a solid and coherent ground of theoretical thinking. It is fair to say that Gaffney has laboured the rich ground from which his thinking on groups has emerged and outlines this clearly to his readers. Informed by existential philosophy, religion, cross-cultural studies, field theory and other aspects of Gestalt psychotherapy, the author presents an attractive and different lens through which to view working with groups. One that breaks with the ethnocentric and predominantly Anglo-American view of group development as a sequence of pre-determined stages through which a group transitions on its way towards a better, more effective and higher performing state. Rather, this book explores a holistic, relational and more phenomenological perspective of an emergent group that is always the best possible version of itself at any moment of its emergence.

In the many vignettes of his work with multi-cultural and diverse groups, I found myself resonating with the uncertainty, novelty and surprise that comes with working within a culture that challenges my sense of 'how things should be'. I was reminded of a time, in my early days of consulting, when a group of middle-eastern university lecturers confounded my colleague by their reluctance to publicly identify the stage of their group process on a pre-determined model of group development. It is only when my colleague understood that the risk of shaming each other was greater than any benefit gained by identifying their status quo as a group, that he could proceed with facilitating dialogue accepting that certain aspects of the group process will remain un-named but nevertheless understood. Practitioners who work across cultures or with multi-cultural groups will find in Gaffney's cross-cultural perspectives a rudder to help navigate these often uncertain waters. The author clearly states that this book is for *"those practitioners who share my dissatisfaction with the socio-cultural limitations of traditional group theories and models"* and as such this book needs to be celebrated for its distinctive offering of an approach that supports facilitators to meet groups in their uniqueness and allow for their emergent development.

The author refers to himself as a practitioner/theorist interweaving theory, practice and resulting methodology. All three are best understood as a totality in context and relationship with each other. As such the book is the product of a phenomenological and hermeneutic research and development process in the sense that it emerges from a lifetime of personal as well as work experience and thinking. Phenomenological research is a lived experience for researchers as they attune themselves to a particular phenomenon (groupwork in this case) with awareness of their pre-reflective, taken-for-granted understandings and prejudices. And so, by acknowledging the embedded-ness of his approach and methodology in his own life experience, Gaffney invites us as readers to reflect on our own journeys, what informs us in our practice and how therefore we stand in relation to a group. As facilitators of groups our personal history, culture and experience is always a part of the field and background (or sometimes even figure) to emerging group situations.

The last part of the book provides examples of the author's workgroup practice which illuminates further his theory and methodologies. What I found most valuable is that in the practical 'how' of his approach to an open group or organisational work, we can witness the author's commitment and respect for the group. Although he does not make it explicit, he conveys, as a group facilitator, a deeply ethical stance; one which is not swayed by the desire to please but rather prioritises the group's emergent process, learning and presence.

This book is intended as a resource rather than an instruction manual. Whilst it is certainly easy to read and provides many inspiring and practical examples of working with groups, it is not a beginner's book. To fully appreciate the depth of the author's offering and experience requires some understanding of the limitations and restrictions of existing theories of group and team work. Furthermore, Gaffney introduces us to *field attunement* as the art and craft of the group facilitator in working from a field perspective. Any facilitator will recognise here the on-going journey of self-development and practice required to reach such levels of skill and expertise.

Gaffney writes with passion and enthusiasm about his work with groups and the vignettes reveal the strength of relationship he establishes with his clients

I think that regardless of the author's warning that it is not for the faint-hearted, you will enjoy this book. It is a compelling read for anyone interested in learning more about the theory and practice of working with groups and about themselves!

Dr. Marie-Anne Chidiac
1 August 2013
Broummana, Lebanon

Opening Statement of Intent

Please check which of the following categories you feel you mostly belong to or maybe even aspire to, both professionally in general and also specifically with regard to groups:

Practitioner (hands-on doing)
Practitioner/Researcher (doing and exploring)
Practitioner/Theorist (doing, reflecting, writing then doing)
Methodologist (how to do)
Theorist (thinking about what to do and hypothesizing on how to do it)

I describe myself as a Practitioner/Theorist inasmuch as I like my practice to be informed and guided by solid theory just as much as I like my practice to add to and subtract from my theory. I feel most excited though not necessarily most comfortable when theory and practice are in flux, and a new methodology is emerging from the interplay of theory and practice. So a Practitioner/Theorist with a strong flavor of Methodologist.

Consistent with these aspects of my work, this book contains theory, methodology and practice. The theory usually comes first in each chapter. Methodology appears mainly in the vignettes offered as examples. These vignettes are indicated in the Table of Contents. "Implications for Practice" in each chapter are just that

– a focus on practice informed by the theory and supported by the methodology.

My suggestion therefore is that the reader picks and chooses where to focus and in what order if any to read each chapter. The book is intended as a resource, not an instruction manual.

Another statement of my intent is that this book is intended to give you, the leader an opportunity to reflect on how you "see" things in general (your perspective), how you interpret the behavior of others (your learned and/or acquired values and judgements), how you understand and acknowledge your own behavior (your self-awareness) and how you regard and relate to others (your relational stance).

I am offering you a sideways shift maybe from a sense of obligation that you, as person/facilitator/manager/leader, will get "them" (the group) to be where "they" should be or to where you as manager (or your manager) want "them" to be. My focus is rather on what you may learn about yourself, others, and the relationships between you – both social and functional – which you can then use as a support for an understanding of the complexity and unpredictability of your task in order to support you do it the best and most creative way you – and only you -can.

This is a shift from a controlled structure to a dynamic process; from management of operations to leadership of professionals as persons and as functional roles; from planned and pre-determined change to organic and emergent change.

I can agree: not a journey for the fainthearted or for those who need certainties. It is a journey for you who live constant change rather than talk about it, see change as referring to yourself also and not just or only to others less powerful or influential than you are in your functional role.

Explanatory Reader Notes

- This book uses an approach called "intersectionality". According to McCall, intersectionality is a research methodology of studying "the relationships among multiple dimensions and modalities of social relationships and subject formations". Accordingly, I introduce philosophy, religion, cross-cultural studies, field theory, social psychology and group theory and all the while weaving my personal and professional experience and practice into the rich patterns that emerge, giving them depth and substance. Other areas of social importance and relevance to groups, such as gender, race, class and power differentials, for example, I am happy to leave to others more experienced and qualified than I in those areas of study. My hope is that people with such competence may find some inspiration here in these pages to add what they regard as missing.

- End of chapter "References and Further Reading" lists will cover literature inspirational for or directly relevant to the content of that chapter, and will be grouped under headings for easy recognition as chapter themes. These replace in-text citations in parentheses and are intended to allow the text to flow more naturally.

- Every hypothesis presented, or abstraction transformed into a construct, or theory proposed as an explanation, is always under the implicit heading: AS

IF. So it will be AS IF a team has three dimensions, AS IF there are three groups in a room simultaneously, AS IF person and role are both integrated as a whole as well as distinguishable as specific aspects of that wholeness.

Literature:

McCall, Leslie. "The Complexity of Intersectionality." Journal of Women in Culture and Society 30.02005 1771–1800 26 Nov 2007

http://www.journals.uchicago.edu/doi/pdf/10.1086/426800

Olsson, J (2011). *Managing Intersectionality - A Gestalt Approach.* Unpublished doctoral thesis, due to the author's illness and death.

Zander, Zander, Gaffney & Olsson (2010). Intersectionality as a new perspective in international business research. *Scandinavian Journal of Management.*

Who and What

My Personal and Professional Background, and an Introduction to this book

Background:
For many years, I much preferred actually working with groups to writing about working with groups. "Working with groups" for me covers all the various applications of my personal and professional life, which are many and various. My life and work include:
- born into and raised in a working-class family in Dublin, Ireland
- completed my secondary school education in Dublin
- novice in a Cistercian monastery in Ireland
- post office sorter/postman in Ireland
- transport clerk in Ireland
- student psychiatric nurse in England
- Marks & Spencer warehouseman in England
- cinema cleaner in England
- front-of-house manager, Irish travelling repertory theatre company
- builder's labourer in Scotland
- scaffolder in Scotland
- domestic appliance service department clerk in England
- service office manager in England
- fitted kitchen salesman in England

- marketing and distribution manager for a kitchen importer in Ireland
- teacher of English as a Foreign language in Sweden
- Department Head, Languages and Professional Communication at the Stockholm School of Economics, Sweden
- Senior Lecturer in Cross-cultural Management and International Organisational Behaviour at Business schools in Stockholm, Riga and Milan
- Diploma in Gestalt psychotherapy (Gestalt Academy of Scandinavia)
- Diploma in Gestalt Organisational Development (Gestalt Institute of Cleveland)
- PhD at the University of Derby (On Borders and Boundaries – Gestalt at Work in a Multicultural World)
- Author – collected papers in two volumes (see references)

Currently:
Gestalt Psychotherapist, trainer and clinical supervisor, individual and group
Gestalt OD Practitioner, trainer and supervisor, individual and group
Full Member, New York Institute for Gestalt Therapy
Senior Professional Associate, Gestalt International Study Center, Cape Cod
Associate, Gestalt Centre Belfast
Faculty, Gestalt Academy of Scandinavia

Guest Faculty:
Nordic Gestalt Institute, Denmark
Norwegian Gestalt Institute, Oslo
Illawarra Gestalt Centre, Wollongong, Australia

So, yes: been there, done that, have a large collection of t-shirts. And it all began – that is, I began as the first-born son in a lower working class Dublin family with an alcoholic butcher father and a lower middle class mother. So it's been kind of uphill since then, and, like a tree, I have both grown from my original roots and also grown new roots on my way.

*****

My foray into publication in professional journals in the early years of this century was an exciting challenge and a rewarding experience. I discovered that I "knew" more than I had thought I knew (though not always exactly where it had come from!) and also that I had a contribution to make to theoretical thinking on the subjects concerned, and also a contribution to method and practice. I then experienced how much my practice was being influenced by my writing. New perspectives and insights occurred regularly as I drafted and revised papers and these then became embodied in my practice. I had moved from doing it to writing about it, back to doing it - and here-and-now to writing about doing it!

And, as I write now, I find myself thinking about groups and all of those of which I have been a member and others with which I have been involved as facilitator or manager or observer throughout my life:

I was born into an extended Irish Catholic family, and thus became a Gaffney, Irish and Catholic without any say in the matter. As the eldest son/grandson, I also became a manager/leader of yet-to-be-born younger sisters and cousins, my duties delegated to me by my parents, grandparents and what seemed like an army of aunties, as well as the ghost of my namesake uncle and mother's brother, dead at fifteen of tuberculosis two years before I was born.

And then there was the Richmond Avenue gang on the street where I lived and grew up, from age two to age 18. We terrorized anyone of the Tolka Road gang who dared to attempt a short cut along their bank of OUR river, the Tolka in Fairview, Dublin. We were, in turn, terrorized by the East Wall gang any time we attempted to use THEIR park, Fairview Park.

We were also a highly successful shoplifting gang, specializing in Woolworths (as I now suspect all Dublin schoolboy shoplifting gangs had as their hunting ground of choice!). A particularly exciting aspect of this was the father of one of us – Tommy – was a retired policeman who was the floorwalker, or security man, for Woolworths. So we had to dodge him as well as the staff.

Because of our various ages, we were in different school classes throughout our schooldays and also had different interests, so I was soon experiencing the complexities of multiple group memberships, without knowing that this was what I was doing.

I finished secondary school in June and became a novice monk in a Cistercian monastery in Ireland in August of the same year, leaving the groups of my street, of my school and of my friendships for the enclosed silent group of a novitiate within a monastery. This was my introduction to community…and my first aware experience of being in a sub-group embedded in a larger whole of sub-groups, each formally bounded in various ways, including the colours of the habits we wore and even our haircuts, the difference in vocation between brothers and priests and the status distinctions between novices, postulants and monks.

Before the two years of my novitiate were over, my novice-master, abbot and prior had reached the conclusion that whilst I seemed maybe right for the monastic life, the monastic life was not right for me. Their recommendation was that I might consider becoming a teacher and maybe even joining a teaching order if I wanted to be a priest…I had no interest in either at the time, and returned to a Richmond Avenue with not one of the old gang still living there. I now joined a group of my old school-friends before emigrating.

After two years as a student psychiatric nurse in England, followed by a period as warehouseman with a Marks & Spencer south London store, I moved between Ireland and England as a very peripheral figure on the edge of the folk music revival in and across both countries. This involved the dynamics of the various allegiances involved – from fundamentalist purists to underground folk-rock.

I then spent a summer season as front-of-house manager and bit actor with an Irish repertory company, my first real experience of a work-group dependent upon individual skills, a high level of interaction and a shared effort in order to achieve collective success. It was during that summer that I met my future Swedish wife…

…and so found myself living in London and working, thanks to the local Labour Exchange, first as service clerk and then as department manager of telephonists and clerks in an Italian domestic appliance company…and then – trainer of new staff. And so I had become a teacher without realizing it at the time or its significance in my life. And then in and out of various companies as middle manager and staff trainer, then management trainer, language teacher, university lecturer and all the rest that I have become.

From group member, to group manager and trainer, to university lecturer, to Gestalt psychotherapist, group therapist, trainer and facilitator…or, from group to group to group, and in various capacities! As such, the statements, opinions and perspectives I offer here are simply confident expressions of where I am in my current practice, based on nearly seventy years of learning, training and hands-on experience of living and working in and with groups.

Introduction

This book is for group practitioners, people who live and work in and/or manage, lead or facilitate groups in any and all ways. It is especially for those practitioners who share my dissatisfaction with the socio-cultural limitations of traditional group theories and models, and who want to join me at the cutting edge of our work in an increasingly multicultural social and organizational environment.

Grounded in all of my considerable reading on the subject, as well as my broad international practice, I have increasingly become convinced the mainstream Anglo-American models and methodologies usually and so habitually applied to groups and group leadership are restricted in their value to an Anglo-American socio-cultural setting. In addition, that the imposition of these approaches on others as mainstream thinking is a form of cultural imperialism. As an Irishman, born into a partitioned nation deprived of its native language and literature by such imperialism, I am allergic to any and all variations of this socio-cultural imposition. Accordingly, I have worked my way through and out of the constraints of these models, and sought a freestanding, more ethnocentrically unencumbered and flexible theory and methodology for my own work with groups internationally. So there is a sense in which my approach here is, in this context, openly political.

And by this, I do not mean some indiscriminate embrace of something called "democracy": I mean a respectful curiosity about my similarities with and distinctions from others, my discovery that what is "right" for me can be "wrong" for another and vice versa. And I do not either mean some idealized, compromised accommodation. I include the misunderstandings for which I am responsible, the knee-jerk reactions of which I am capable – and the sorting out that may or may not be possible. It is this openness and ability to work at sorting out our tangles that is at the heart of living and working in a multicultural world.

What I am proposing here is a theoretical base and methodology for the multi-cultural, multi-ethnic, multi-faith groups of the 21st. century, with examples from my practice for group facilitators, managers and OD consultants.

As I have said earlier, I see myself as a practitioner-theorist with an attraction to methodology. Whilst I am always happy to sense how theory informs and supports practice, I am always excited when my practice further informs theory and may even change it.

Indeed, drafting this book has provided me with an example of my practice informing theory. To begin with, I no longer use any of the Anglo-American models in any socio-cultural environment other that from which they come – England and the U.S.A. Secondly, I no longer use the terms group "development" or "phases" or "stages" but rather group "change" or "evolution" or even "emergent group". I find these more congruent both with insights from my international experience as well as my preferred philosophical perspective and current methodology.

My philosophical base is existentialism, which is more a way of living than a theory, though it includes a broad knowledge-base (see below). Gestalt psychology is another source of inspiration for my thinking, both in its original form as a theory of perception and learning, and also in one of it's more unlikely offshoots, Gestalt psychotherapy. Each and both of these move me into the area of methodology, and most specifically into field theory. In terms of theory and method, I work and write from a Gestalt field perspective including phenomenology in its influence on Existentialism as well as its value as a methodology in itself (see recommended reading).

I work in two languages – English and Swedish, and my Swedish gets me by in Denmark and Norway. I have regularly worked on five continents plus the Middle East. As a practitioner-theorist, I am in favour of being fully who I am while at the same time fully respecting the socio-cultural environments in which I find myself, and dealing with the tensions which arise in the service of my relationship with whatever group is involved. I believe that this is a growing theme for the century in which we now find ourselves – taking responsibility for the differences between us, appreciating our similarities, and creatively using the tensions that arise to find new ways of meeting at the porous and dynamic interfaces which are the emergent creations of our meetings, in all their complexity.

I have explored the above themes in various papers published in peer-review journals, some of which also appeared in my successful doctoral submission in 2009, when, at the age of 67, I became an OAPh.D! (OAP in Ireland and England is the standard acronym for Old Age Pensioner!). This book is intended as a statement of my current thinking, as my professional careers and my personal life near their closing.

I regard myself as a well-informed and experienced fellow-practitioner to my readers. Or, to put it more precisely: a practitioner-theorist. As such, a continuous cycle of inductive-deductive processes keeps my practice up-to-date with my thinking and my thinking challenged and refreshed by my practice.

It is this learning loop that I want to explore here as well as its consequences for a theory, methodology and practice of groupwork free from the encumbrances of the established ethnocentric theories and models – a theory, methodology and practice for an increasingly multicultural, multiethnic and multi-faith population.

I approach therapeutic, educational, organizational and social settings as the natural habitat of a humanistic, socially congruent approach to groups. After all, groups, along with the family, form our basic context as social animals and also as social beings with a philosophy and a psychology. A core theme of the book is that our social relations as human beings will be the ever-present ground for such specific foreground figures as training groups, work groups, teams, associations, communities, organizations and whole societies. My interest is in the interplay between the relational (people as a Social Group), the functional (roles in a Work Group), and the shared task-oriented (people and roles as an integrated whole in a Team). This theme is more fully explicated below.

Finally, this book deepens and broadens the theory and practice of group-work by explicitly including the influences of such disciplines as cross-cultural studies, philosophy and social psychology, and a broad international experience of participating in, managing, leading and facilitating groups of many kinds in many places over a lifetime.

The book is organized as a series of focused, thematic sections covering concepts, methodology - and practice where possible and useful. Each section has emerged as relevant from the wholeness of my knowledge and experience, at the same time as they and you, the reader, form a unique whole in the complex matrix of your connecting and interacting with the material of the book.

While it is a cliché that "the map is not the territory", this has not dissuaded mapmakers from their trade, nor travellers from using maps. Since this is a book, then it has more in common with a printed map than with a Sat-Nav, for example. So, yes: see this book as a map…and as a map of MY group territory. One purpose of this book is to encourage readers to use my map to take them to where they get to, where they then design their own maps for their own group work territory.

Welcome to the wonderful world of groups!

References and Recommended Reading

By the Author:

Gaffney, S. (2009). On Borders and Boundaries – Gestalt at Work in a Multicultural World. Successful Ph.D submission, University of Derby, England.

Gaffney, S. (2008/2011). Gestalt at Work – Integrating Life, Theory and Work. Collected Papers Volumes 1 & 2. Metairie, LA, USA, Gestalt Institute Press.

Volume 1 contains "On Finding My Way" a paper on my journey from Cistercian novice to teacher, trainer and author.

Volume 2 contains "In Transition", also cited below.

A Gestalt Field Perspective

O'Neill & Gaffney (2008). Field Theoretical Strategy. Handbook for Theory, Research and Practice in Gestalt Therapy. Philip Brownell, Editor. Cambridge Scholars Publishing. Newcastle, England.

Fairfield, Mark (2004). Gestalt Groups Revisited: A Phenomenological Approach. Gestalt Review, Vol. 8/3. Gestalt International Study Center, Wellfleet MA, USA.

Staemmler, Frank M. (2006). A Babylonian Confusion – The Term 'Field'. British Gestalt Journal, 15, 2, Bristol, England.

The journey from Practitioner to Practitioner-Researcher to Practitioner-Theorist:

Gaffney, S. (2011). In Transition…with commentaries by Brownell, P; Congram, S; and Mistler, B. Gstalt! Electronic journal of AAGT.

Some Philosophical Considerations

The Existential Dilemma

Philosophers from Kierkegaard and Nietzsche to Buber and Levinas, to Husserl, Stein, Heidegger, Sartre, Merleau-Ponty, Marcel, Tillich and Jaspers have explored what I am choosing here to call "The Existential Dilemma" – a sense of being a part of social units with other people, or alternatively a sense of being apart from them. Examples of such "social units" are called friends, couples, families, groups, organizations, religions or even societies. And also whether the person concerned has a sense of agency in a subjective choice, or a sense of being the object of the choice of others. For Kierkegaard and Nietzsche, this was the challenge for the existing individual faced with the demands of any anonymous social mass – society in general for Nietzsche, and the established Danish church and middle-class Copenhagen for Kierkegaard.

Kierkegaard wonderfully captured the paradox of the existential dilemma: while relentlessly supporting the notion of "the existing individual", he could also write: "Deep within every man there lies the dread of being alone in the world, forgotten by God, overlooked among the tremendous household of millions and millions. That fear is kept away by looking upon all those about one who are bound to one as friends or family, but the dread is nevertheless there and one hardly dares to think of what would happen to one of us if all the rest were taken away."

While Nietzsche could proclaim that "God is dead" and thus open the door for the free, unencumbered individual to take her place in the world – on her own terms as a human being – Kierkegaard had the existence of God as a given around which the individual needed to make choices. In his many and various writings, he explored the choices, their consequences, their ambiguities, their paradoxes and their existential challenges. He introduced the notion of "anxiety" as an existential quality, calling it "the dizziness of freedom".

Nietzsche and Kierkegaard also represent the two major strands of European existentialism – Nietzsche the atheistic and Kierkegaard the theistic. American existentialism can be represented by a humanistic perspective, one which regards the existence or otherwise of a God to be secondary to the existence of humans. Humanistic existentialism is an aspect of the human potential movement, usually associated with the work of Abraham Maslow and a major paradigm in the U.S.A from the 1950's onwards. These themes are further explored in Chapter 5 below.

Theistic existentialists such as Kierkegaard, Buber, Marcel, Tillich and Jaspers brought God into the equation, and as such, the meaning of life in relation to belief in the existence of God. Believing in the existence of God still leaves open the question of what a person is to do about it. Kierkegaard maintained and developed his belief in God, while insisting on freeing himself from the constraints and dogmatism of the established Danish protestant church. He always regarded himself as a Christian facing the dilemmas of being an existing individual in a social environment. The same can be said of Marcel, Tillich and Jaspers.

Buber was a Hasidic Jew whose philosophical thinking took God as a given, and who proposed the divine can become manifest in open, vulnerable and fully mutual meetings between people. His emphasis was on "can" become manifest. We can never know in advance; any attempt to "make" it happen is a guaranteed failure. The divine becomes manifest on Its own terms, not ours. Within the context of its spiritual perspective, Buber's approach to being human is both intensely relational and intensely spiritual.

The atheistic existentialists , such as Heidegger, Sartre, de Beauvoir, Merleau-Ponty and Levinas, for example, see us as born into or even "thrown" into a world already here before us and probably still here after we have died: so there is no inherent "meaning of life" other than to live our lives in the face of this meaninglessness, and give it momentary meaning through the choices we make in our own responsibility for ourselves and our own existence as we travel towards the non-experience of no longer existing.

Heidegger and Levinas explored the presence of "the other" in different ways. For Levinas, the presence of the other created a humanistic ethical context for our being and behaviour. For Heidegger, our "being-with-others" is intrinsic to our "being-in-the-world", it is simply "there", a fact of being which we have no option but to deal with while we – and others - happen to be around.

So: for Buber, the mutuality of meeting "the other" in what he famously called an "I – Thou" moment allowed the presence of the divine to emerge in that instant. Equally famously, Sartre declared that "hell is other people". In the U.S.A, Maslow would propose that self-realisation is the developmental pinnacle of a life well lived, including the willingness to support the development of others.

Whichever of these perspectives we feel is congruent for us, existentialism is firmly rooted in the paradox of being alone in our experience of our existence in the company of others similarly preoccupied with being here, in and of the world, knowing that death is always just around the next corner, with or without an afterlife of some kind.

This brief summary of existentialism can be further summarized in some of the everyday phrases we use to express these complex ideas:

"I just need to be alone."

"You need to get out and meet people."

"I'm worried about my son – he doesn't seem to have any friends."

"They go everywhere together – they're inseparable."

"She never had her own interests or friends – so when he left her, she had no-one to turn to."

A particular aspect of existentialism as a philosophy is the manner in which it became associated with literature. In Europe, the novels of Dostoevsky, Sartre and Camus, and the plays of Sartre and Becket all explore and or describe an existential perspective on life – and death.

In the USA, writers like Steinbeck and Hemingway, and later, Rhinehart, explored aspects of the existential in their work.

This literary aspect of existentialism as a philosophy has become embedded in the English-speaking world as less an academic philosophy and more a way of life, of living in the world and dealing with our mortality. This is, perhaps, one of the particular contributions of existentialism: a way of thinking so congruent with our lives that it became easily integrated and naturally expressed in literature of the highest quality.

And also in a very special genre: that of the thriller or crime fiction. Authors like Dashiell Hammet, Jim Thompson and later Walter Mosley, James Sallis and James Lee Burke have all explored the shadowy world at the edge of society, where social norms have little or no impact and existence is a form of personal integrity.

From Philosophy to Social Psychology

And so to the gradual shift from philosophy to psychology, beginning perhaps in Germany with Brentano in the late 1800's, including the work of Freud and the contribution of psychoanalysis, and culminating in the work of the Gestalt psychologists, Wertheimer, Koffka and Köhler, for whom knowledge was subjective, created in the interplay of people experiencing an event and the meaning-making process of each person as they transform that experience into knowledge. This was already a significant shift from the purely intra-psychic processes of the Freudian individual in a vacuum.

Kurt Lewin, well-acquainted with Gestalt psychology, had moved from controlled psychological experiments in the laboratory in the Germany of the 1920s to more socially-situated research studies, especially following his arrival in the USA in 1933. As such, he became the acknowledged father of social psychology. He also became the father of Action Learning and Action Research. For Lewin, the meaning of any behavior could be found in the interplay between a person and her environment as she perceives it. As such, behavior was an expression of the meaning a person made of their perceived environment, and the action which resulted. We behave in what he called the life space, that is, us embedded in our physical and social environments. We behave according to our understanding and our needs, including the adjustments and compromises we make.

For psychoanalyst Helen Durkin, Lewin created the bridge from the individual to the social. Behaviour became interpersonal, or, as contemporary psychoanalysts say – intersubjective. The environmental other was now involved in my world and our behaviours were in relation to each other. For Durkin, Lewin's work opened the door for psychoanalysts into groups and organizations – the social environments of our significant behaviors. As the founding father of The National Training Laboratory (NTL), an institute dedicated to research into groups and the practice of group-work, Kurt Lewin has left a lasting impression on this field. This includes his influence on the Tavistock Institute in London and its psychodynamic explorations of groups, organizations and leadership.

As social psychology developed as a distinct discipline, the importance of our social environments in forming who we are – our identity, our sense of self – became a subject of interest. Social psychologists now talk about the self as a characteristic of an individual person; or emergent from the relations we have with others, continuously changing in a dynamic relational dance; or a specific expression of a collective self which we all both share and co-create.

Social Identity Theory (SIT) is a particular branch of social psychology devoted to exploring the social nature of our identity, giving a research-based academic foundation to a common citation from Martin Buber to the effect that I become me through my meeting with you, and you become you through your meeting with me. We are both recognizably ourselves over time while becoming ourselves uniquely now also in the moment of each meeting.

While the extent to which each one of us has a sense of a distinct and discrete self is socio-culturally and also philosophically and religiously informed, the facts of our social and functional work roles are less open to interpretation. Our social roles include being children, grandchildren, siblings, relatives, parents and grandparents, neighbours, friends. Professionally, we are managers, subordinates, colleagues, doctors, salesmen, teachers etc.

Together, these create three domains of an individual's existence: the private, the personal and the professional, all situated in a socio-cultural and/or socio-organizational context. In some contexts, these three domains will generally be seen as discrete aspects of a person's life, best kept apart; in other contexts, any distinctions between them will be played down.

Kurt Lewin gives a graphic example of these two perspectives, using avocadoes as a metaphor to illustrate typical German and U.S.A attitudes. In Lewin's example, the green flesh is the socially open and available parts of a person's life, and the nut is the less available, more closed private aspects. He writes that the typical German avocado has very little flesh and a large, hard nut. The typical U.S.A avocado has masses of flesh and a small, almost impenetrable nut.

Implications for Practice

All of the ideas raised above come together and are enacted in groups as gatherings of social animals and thinking, feeling beings – whether or not they are also parents, CEOs, salespersons, accountants, footballers, students or whatever.

It is not unusual in the lifetime of any group that a member will be dealing with a birth, an illness, a death, a divorce, a marriage, a promotion, a dismissal, a troubled child, sibling, spouse or relative, or any other of the myriad of existential issues that simply being alive entails. There are always those who believe that such issues are their own business and do not belong to the life of the group. This attitude is most common in work-groups in commercial organisations. And yet, work-groups are usually embedded in organizations where the numbers of people involved increase the possibility of the impact of such existential issues. To claim that a recently bereaved person in a department, or someone going through a difficult divorce, is not impacting on work colleagues and friends and therefore in one way or another on the whole department, and by extension, the whole organization, is missing the point of being human as being primarily socially situated.

A trendy platitude in the workplace is that "everything changes" – with the exception, it seems, of people, who are expected to be predictably the same from day to day, largely perhaps, in order to be "manageable". So yes! Everything does change, including us. And we change in relation to each other, we behave in relation to each other, just as we are impacted as persons AND as functions in our workplaces by events in our own and others' private and personal lives outside of the workplace.

In consequence, whenever I have a group of any kind which meets regularly, I will generally open a session by asking if there are any factual circumstances which have changed for anyone since we last met in a way that they would like us to know. This at least provides an opportunity for a member to share information with us, and, since my invitation is repeated at each meeting after the first one, then members can actually prepare themselves to say something if they wish.

In any event, the opportunity is always there for the wholeness of our lives, inside and outside the group, to be available to all as individual grist for our collective mill.

This brings me to the opportunity to provide a preliminary introductory summary of my perspective on and approach to groups: any gathering of human beings is primarily and always a social context from which other specific considerations can emerge, such as a therapy group, a school class, a business project group, a football team, a commando unit in an army, for example. There is also the socio-cultural aspect of how gatherings of people in any cultural setting are expected to behave towards each other, including as independent individuals, as family, clan or tribal members, or as group members embedded in the group-as-a-whole of our socio-cultural context.

Vignette 1, Singapore

A vignette here may support an understanding of what can be involved in holding such a perspective and approach: I am engaged by a young Singapore Chinese male CEO to meet with his Executive Management Team in Singapore. He is the son of the founder who recently retired and handed over the organization to his eldest son, as one does amongst the Singapore Chinese. He has an MBA from a prestigious American university and has an excellent grasp of organizational terminology in its US dialect. In line with this, I ask him what he wants. He replies with what "we" need, "we" being the organization. Clearly, whilst he has picked up the dialect of individualism, his natural inclination is to represent the collective.

He tells me that "we" need a better understanding of organizational development issues and how to deal with them. He respectfully requests that I meet the Executive Management Team and support them with their issues, so that their understanding can cascade down though the organisation. He makes it clear that he will not attend, as his presence would mean that they were unlikely to speak out. "This isn't the States!" he adds.

So I meet them, all of them Singapore Chinese ranging in age from 30-ish to 60-ish, both male and female. The elder amongst them let me know that they have previously worked for the father and have stayed in the organization at the father's request (even if "request" may not be an accurate description in Western terms). After the lengthy preliminaries so natural in Asia, there comes an acknowledgement that they are clearly a problem for the CEO. I state that Mr. Chang (let's call him that) has respectfully allowed me to meet them without any demands either on me or on them to do anything other than support the best functioning of the organization. He has certainly not described them to me as a "problem" – which is, of course, a "nuancing" of the situation that I might not try in another socio-cultural context.

We have a pleasant lunch with a conversational focus on me answering their curiosities about Ireland where I come from, and Sweden where I live.

After lunch, there is the magical moment of what I call a "shift", a slight though perceptible movement from one position to another. I am asked if I know the Myers Briggs Type instrument. I do, so now comes information on how Mr. Chang gave them all an MBTI folder and that they filled it in and shared it with each other and with him, even though it was difficult for them to do so at times. We discussed the use and value of personality tests.

And then it came: the issue for them as they experienced it. Mr. Chang had also given them the FIRO folder on group developmental phases. He was very disappointed with them that they had not had any conflicts among the team, typical of Phase 2 - CONTROL - which meant that they could not move on to the next and final phase of their development.

I know of Asia as a socio-cultural setting where open internal conflict in a group is countercultural in many respects – in and of itself anyway, between generations and genders certainly, between senior and junior executives of course and still many more such considerations than I can even imagine. The fact that this is, in Western eyes, a "work group" is largely incidental, and probably entirely secondary in existential, socio-cultural terms to its members.

So I choose to "nuance" again, all within the subtleties of the setting – I hope! I suggest that there would seem to be a conflict between the Executive Management Team and Mr. Chang on this issue, since they are clearly not doing what he expects and that this conflict has been so well handled by both parties – them and him – that no damage has been done either to the organization or the relationship and that they are now free to develop further with a shared experience of tension as a firm foundation.

There are smiles all round. My work is done.

This is an example of a socio-culturally appropriate intervention which seems to have achieved something. These interventions require a combination of knowledge, sensitivity and curiosity available to anybody interested in working multi-culturally.

My point is this: approaching this situation exclusively as an organizational issue and concerned only with the functions and duties of some illusion of a generic and instrumentally perfect Executive Management Team would have missed the socio-cultural and existential richness of the complexities involved.

This vignette also sets the scene for Chapters 4 and 5 which follow...

References

Existentialism:

Atterton, Calarco & Friedman, Editors. (2004). *Levinas & Buber – Dialogue and Difference.* Duquesne University Press, Pittsburgh PE, USA.

Becker, E. (1973). *The Denial of Death.* Free Press Paperbacks, New York.

Blackham, H.J. (1952): *Six Existentialist Thinkers.* Routledge & Kegan Paul, London. England.

Cooper, David E. (1999): *Existentialism.* Blackwell. Oxford, England.

Hubben, William, (1952). *Dostoevsky, Kierkegaard, Nietzsche & Kafka.* Simon & Schuster. New York.

Marino. Gordon (editor): *Basic Writings of Existentialism.* The Modern Library, New York, U.S.A.

Maslow, Abraham H. (1968). *Toward a Psychology of Being.* Reinhold Company, New York.

May, Rollo. Editor. (1961). *Existential Psychology.* McGraw Hill, New York.

Tillich, P. (1952). *The Courage to Be.* Collins. London, England.

Social Identity Theory:

Sedikides, C. and Brewer, M. B., Editors (2001). *Individual self, Relational self, Collective self.* Philadelphia, Psychology Press.

Gestalt Psychology:

Ellis, Willis D., Editor (1997). *A Source Book of Gestalt Psychology.* Gestalt Journal Press, Highland NY, USA.

Perls, Hefferline & Goodman (1951). *Gestalt Therapy – Excitement and Growth in the Human Personality.* The Guernsey Press, Guernsey Islands.

Kurt Lewin:

Gold, M. (Editor). (1999), *The Complete Social Scientist - A Kurt Lewin Reader.* American Psychological Association, Washington.

Marrow, A.J. (1969). *The Practical Theorist – The Life and Work of Kurt Lewin.* New York, NY. Basic Books.

Durkin, Helen E. (1964). *The Group in Depth.* New York NY. International Universities Press, Inc

Lewin, K. (1997). *Resolving Social Conflicts and Field Theory in Social Science.* Washington DC. American Psychological Association

Field Perspectives

Introduction

The inclusion in Chapter 3 of national culture (Singapore Chinese) as an influence on individual and group behaviour, whether known or acknowledged by the people concerned, is already bringing a field perspective into consideration here.

Kurt Lewin borrowed freely from modern physics to extrapolate a field theory of human behavior. Two aspects of physics in particular: the electromagnetic field, undeniably there as evidenced by its influence, though invisible; and vectors – energies or forces with an origin, direction and magnitude. Our contemporary analogy for an electromagnetic field is WiFi. We only really know it is there/here when we open our devices and get a signal – we know it exists through its influence on our devices. We can then assume that it existed before we opened our devices, and after we closed them...though this can only be an assumption.

The same analogy can be used for vectors: the WiFi energy has its nearest relevant origin in a nearby router and is multi- and/or non-directed until we open a receiving device – then the direction is clearly established. And as we know, the signal strength (magnitude) can vary.

As socio-cultural beings, we are living receivers for the signals of our social environment, its history, traditions, norms and expectations of us as members. We are each of us of the field of energies which combine in repeated and recognizable patterns over time to be our culture. For some of us, it can be liberating to travel out of our home culture and get a sense of being able to behave more as we would choose than as we should; for others, such a thought is confusing enough to be impossible to hold.

In the Singapore vignette, Mr. Chang, a privileged Number One son, had the freedom to move from the field of Singapore Chinese culture to a number of years in a prestigious U.S. business school - a specific energy of the field of the U.S. cultural environment. He returned, possibly seeing himself as a vector of change and innovation, directed at his senior executives. Despite the strength of his message, his social position and formal power as the founder's son and CEO, this energy was culturally incongruent enough to be deflected off target by the socio-cultural energy of conflict-avoidance, which in itself seems to have been strong enough to dilute and dissipate the energy of incongruent change.

So: a field is both extremely intangible – just as WiFi is – and at the same time, extremely concrete in its impact on us.

Theoretical Distinctions

A Gestalt field perspective encompasses a number of approaches to field theory – from that of ecology through that of social-psychology and then spirituality. For the reader's orientation, these can be listed as follows, along with their sources:

The ECOLOGICAL field – Jan Smuts, Frank Lovelock

The BIOLOGICAL field – Kurt Goldstein

The PSYCHO-BIOLOGICAL field – the Gestalt psychologists, Max Wertheimer, Kurt Koffka, Wolfgang Köhler

The SOCIAL-PSYCHOLOGICAL field – Kurt Lewin

The SPIRITUAL field – Buber, Swedenborg, Wilber

The work of Smuts, Goldstein, Wertheimer, Koffka and Köhler and – to a much lesser extent, Lewin – can be found in what is regarded as the source-book of Gestalt therapy by Perls, Hefferline and Goodman. However, as Staemmler has eloquently and persuasively pointed out, categories and domains of knowledge become entangled there in an undifferentiated confusion of the physiological with the neurological, the emotional with the intellectual. This is what O'Neill and Gaffney attempted to untangle and integrate in what they call a Gestalt Field Perspective, which is very much the root-system from which the small, flowering bush of this book is growing (to mix metaphors even further!).

In the taxonomy above, Ecology here embraces the biological, and is the domain of the organism and its physical environment. The Biological here is that of the wholeness of the individual as a physical organism. The Gestalt psychologists introduced the psychology of perception, beginning with that of the eyes and ears, and then on into cognitive processes of meaning-making. The social-psychological is the domain of what can be called the psycho-organism – the human being – and conceptualized as a person in an environment, whether physical or psychological. The spiritual domain brings us into the transpersonal, where fools rush in and angels love to tread. This is the realm of the inexplicable, of a felt and sensed union of some sort. If you have ever been there, then you have been there, done that and have the t-shirt.

The ecological track has a history about as old as mankind. Everything organic and inorganic in the universe is part of a whole eco-system, with interdependent and connected parts. This is also the contemporary world of Gaia and the butterfly in the Brazilian rain forest whose flapping wings influence a tornado in Arizona. Whilst the Gaia Hypothesis was laughed at by many natural scientists at the time of its presentation in the 1970's, more and more natural sciences are now open to exploring its relevance. The whole issue of global warming is a prime example, where what happens in one sphere of life on earth has an impact on other spheres, from the melting ice of the poles to the present and future fate of polar bears and penguins.

For the purpose of exploring groups and groupwork, such an all-embracing perspective is certainly valid: there will always be events outside of our awareness which may and can influence behavior in groups without any of the parties involved being any the wiser at the time. As Swedenborg famously said: "nothing unconnected ever happens". Here, connectedness is not in some linear cause and effect chain. It is simply connectedness, as in, for example, "coincidence" or "synchronicity". In "Methodology" below I give an example which will illustrate the complexity of the ecological perspective as we move from theory to practice.

The next approach presented here brings us to Lewin's social-psychological field theory in its psychological extrapolation of the new physics as an emerging science. For Lewin (as much as for Einstein), a field is the totality of influences at any given moment which can make behavior understandable in its present expression – for Einstein the behavior of sub-atomic particles, for Lewin the behavior of people. As such, behavior is truly situational. It emerges from a social situation, and is, at the same time, an expression of that situation.

We can certainly understand present behavior with reference to the past as classical Freudian psychoanalysis would have it – with the distinction for Lewin that the past does not explain the present in a determined causal sequence. His focus was on always accepting present behaviours as expressions of a current understanding of a situation and an attempt to move from present to future, with intention (whether realized or not). The intention of a future outcome occurs in the present, and it is in the present that we can find the gestalt of time and space.

Finally, Lewin advised that we delimit our view of any field to that which we can manage, handle, deal with – whatever phrase gives you a sense of agency.

So this is the first theoretical distinction: from the somewhat limitless perspective of an ecological and/or spiritual approach compared with the delimited approach of Lewin's social-psychological perspective which examines the connections that can be experienced and directly traced in the here-and-now of our phenomenal behavioral interactions.

The second distinction has to do with Lewin's own theory, and is in two parts: part 1 is Martin Gold's distinction between the meta-theory – field theory as a theory of creating theory – and field theory as a methodology, as a way of testing a hypothesis. My focus in this book is field theory as a methodology –

not only as a research methodology but also as a methodological practice with groups (see below).

Part 2 involves untangling a knot that Lewin himself helped to tie. He uses two terms – field and life-space – as if they are more interchangeable than they actually came to be – in my considered opinion. Called "The Practical Theorist" by his biographer, Lewin himself I would like to think would approve of my practice-based extrapolations of his constructs.

As abstractions, field and life-space are clearly very similar. Field is "the totality of co-existing facts which are conceived of as mutually interdependent" and which influence the behavior of a person. Life-space is that person's experience of the field – a part's perspective on the whole of which it is a part, and therefore excluding the person herself as a constituent and observable part of the wholeness of the field. That is, the person has little or no ability to consider herself as the origin of any vector and examine its impact in the totality of the field in the abstract.

So, while the "contents" of a field and a life-space would seem to be identical, the first is a description of the totality including the person concerned (field), and the second is the phenomenological experience (life-space) of being that person with a sense of agency in relation to her perceived physical/social environment. We are each of a field, and we are each in a life-space. And that life-space is always of the moment for the person, the perspectival core embedded in all the richness of possibilities emerging from the wholeness of the field of which she is also an intrinsic part.

Lewin had an attraction for mathematical formulae as bearers of his often complex thinking. I have always liked the elegant simplicity of his formula for human behavior:

$$B = f(P, E).$$

Behavior is a function of a person and her environment, that is, a person and what she experiences as her life-space and to which she is relating and responding to in an apparent mix of the proactive and reactive (where even "proactive" is a response). In other words, behavior is the emergent figure of the ground of the person-environment field.

The life-space as the situation of the interpersonal event of the social field was the previously-mentioned breakthrough Durkin referred to when she asserted that Lewin had provided psychoanalysis with an opportunity to also move from the discrete world of the intrapersonal, unrelated individual to the interpersonal, social world into which we are born, where we learn to be who we are and in which we behave as we believe is consistent with our sense of who we are in relation to others.

Implications for Practice

I will open here with a look at what can happen when two of these perspectives - the ecological of Smuts and later Lovelock, and the social-psychological of Lewin - seem to overlap. I'm thinking here of the groups I was working with in Sweden on what is called 9/11, or also in Sweden on the day of the sinking of a ferry in the Baltic with the loss of over 700 lives, most of them Swedish, and of the International Executive MBA group at the Stockholm School of Economics with two members in Thailand at the time of the tsunami. Such events are unique, traumatic in their impact and utterly impossible to undo. As group leaders, all we can do is work with their impact – on individuals, established or new sub-groups and on the whole collective, including, of course, ourselves.

Working with the impact of such events moves the origin of the vectors concerned from the events themselves to the people impacted on. In other words, from the macro perspective of the ecological to the manageable delimited field of Lewin. And also from a field to a life space approach, to acknowledging behaviours in the moment as expressions of a person's understanding of their environments – including the traumatic events – and their attempts to respond.

For the group facilitator, this means not only acknowledging but also validating each of the multiplicity of human responses, by moving from the there-and-then of the event itself, through the there-and-then of its impact as the person concerned experienced it, to the here-and-now of her social interactions in this room and in this group – now - as an expression of this experience.

***

The nuances of field and life-space also have distinct implications for the formally designated group leader, in whatever capacity – therapist, facilitator, manager, for example. There is a collection of people who identify as group members. The formal leader is not a member on equal footing with other members. At one and the same time, the group members together with the formal leader constitute a unified field of energized influences which self-organise and self-regulate. During this process, each person will have a sense of self, of "me" and "not me". For the leader, this "not me" is primarily the group, individually and collectively. "Not me" is the perceived environmental other of the leader, her immediate partner in current and future interpersonal interactions at the interface for her of "me" and "not me".

Methodology – field attunement

I have coined the term field attunement to capture the craft and art of working from an integrated field perspective, transforming theory into methodology and practice.

What follows is my understanding of what field attunement is all about. As it is my understanding, I will describe it in the first person. This will also support me to own and acknowledge my thinking more immediately:

Vignette 2, Sweden

I meet a group of consultants/trainers for a three-day residential OD supervision/coaching group, four times a year. We explore various aspects of supervision, consultancy and coaching. For example, I supervise whatever client work they wish to bring. At times, members will consult to or coach each other. In such cases, the consultant/coach can choose to have direct supervision, with me available in the room as they work; or they can choose to work first with me out of the room, and then have supervision with me after their work, and in plenum. This latter approach allows for fascinating insights into the whole process for all concerned – consultant/coach, client and onlookers. It is truly a field approach to supervision/training, allowing us the opportunity to experience and observe a multiplicity of life spaces as we process our work.

At a recent session, Angela requested supervision on a very difficult and challenging piece of training that she was engaged in at a hospital. Her own first training and profession was nursing, and she was engaged by a hospital HR department to support the planned merger of two clinics into one unit. The doctors concerned were in agreement about the change, but there were some doubts about the attitudes of the nursing staff. She had designed a two-day programme for nurses from the two clinics, with a focus on change processes, communication and co-operation. About halfway into our contracted 45-minute session, I was having difficulties connecting her opening input with where she now seemed to be in her narrative. I asked Angela to describe how she had contracted this work, both with HR, and also with the participants. In asking this question, I might just as well have asked her to explain Einstein's theory of relativity in ten words. She stopped functioning in front of my eyes. She was at a loss for words, her eyes were darting all around me though never at my eyes, she became almost incoherent as she asked me to repeat my question. Realising that my question had evoked such a strong reaction, I back-pedalled and shifted back into asking her to tell me how the programme had gone. She was very pleased with the first day, and very confused by the second. Some participants had not turned up for the second day, and a few of those who did were critical of the content. I asked how general or specific the criticism was...again, Angela seemed to shut down. She said she wanted to stop there, and maybe do more work with me later in the weekend.

Coming down the stairs the next morning to enter the work-room, I could feel an idea forming... and as I opened the session, I suggested to Angela that she consider talking the remainder of the supervision group through her process of contracting, planning and running the programme, without me in the room. She very readily agreed. After I had left, she spent over an hour with her fellow participants, and reported later that this session had really been very good for her, and she could feel how her next meeting with the nurses would be important for her in establishing a good working relationship with them.

That evening, at the dinner table, Angela began talking about her cousin, Birgitta, who she feels doesn't like or respect her. In fact, Birgitta likes to call Angela a "pseudo-psychologist" at family gatherings. Someone asked what Birgitta's profession was. A doctor... and then, with a mixture of disbelief and growing relief – a doctor at the very hospital where Angela was now working as an OD consultant/trainer. Birgitta would be certain to hear of any criticism directed at Angela, which would only confirm her prejudices about her as an OD consultant and trainer – and pseudo-psychologist. Suddenly Angela could see the whole matter in a completely new light. The phrase "elephant in the room" had gone from a trivial cliché to a living example. It was as if Birgitta had been in every room involved: the training room, the supervision room – and now the dining room! The following day Angela presented her new design for the next session at the hospital

My hypothesis here is that Birgitta was the origin of a vector of the Angela – Hospital – Birgitta field. Clearly, she was the origin of a devaluing judgement experienced by Angela as being aimed in her direction, with quite a strong energy – though not acknowledged by Angela other than as a force of the field of Angela's family. And yet as she could acknowledge when I did some teaching about field and life space, criticism as a powerful and impactful force was resonating throughout the whole process of the two-day training – and the supervision session. Her confusion at the nurses' criticism, her confusion at my questions (which, she agreed, she had taken to be questioning her competence) – all evoked her sense of being unseen and unheard by Birgitta except as a pseudo-psychologist of little or no competence or consequence. Angela's sudden understanding of Birgitta's presence as a force of the Angela – Hospital – Birgitta field, brought Birgitta into her awareness as an environmental other previously sensed rather than seen, and now an aware aspect of Angela's life space. She dealt with it quite brilliantly, and brought her work to the following supervision residential.

On her return to the nurses, she opened by apologizing for not having mentioned earlier that she is a trained nurse, and spoke of the hospitals and wards where she had been a Sister. She addressed her own experience of re-organisations, merging wards etc., and then how she had completed a four-year training at diploma level in Gestalt OD. So here she was working with nurses from a new competence on top of her competence and experience as a nurse in hospitals such as the one they were now in...

The emergence of Birgitta and what she represented from a hazy background presence of the field into being a full figure of Angela's life space inspired Angela to establish her competence, on her own terms. She also addressed how important it had been for her to experience her relief at working with her peers in the absence of any authority figures (me, for example) at the previous supervision meeting. My hypothesis here concerns the self-organising and self-regulating of the various fields of which Angela was an energy or force, beginning with the training programme, then from Friday morning (my session with her), to Saturday morning (her peer session), to Saturday night at dinner (Birgitta's appearance), to Sunday morning and her resolve to define and take a stand on her own unique competence. Included here is the energy I felt to spontaneously suggest the peer review and to remove myself from the scene. To coin a phrase: the field is alive with the sound of music. And field attunement supports me to be always tuned in and ready to sing along in harmony, especially with an unknown tune.

References

A Gestalt Field Perspective

Fairfield, Mark (2004). Gestalt Groups Revisited: A Phenomenological Approach. *Gestalt Review, Vol. 8/3.* Gestalt International Study Center. Wellfleet MA, USA.

Gaffney, S & O'Neill, B. (2013). *The Gestalt Field Perspective – Methodology and Practice.* Ravenwood Press, Wollongong, NSW, Australia.

Goldstein, Kurt (2000). *The Organism.* Zone Books, New York.

Köhler, Wolfgang (1969). *The Task of Gestalt Psychology.* Princeton University Press, Princeton.

O'Neill, B & Gaffney; S (2008). Field Theoretical Strategy. *Handbook for Theory, Research and Practice in Gestalt Therapy.* Philip Brownell, Editor. Cambridge Scholars Publishing. Newcastle, England.

Staemmler, Frank M. (2006). A Babylonian Confusion – The Term 'Field'. *British Gestalt Journal,* **15,** 2, Bristol, England.

Smuts, J.C (1998). *Holism and Evolution.* Gestalt Journal Press. Highlands NY, USA.

Wertheimer, Max (1982). *Productive Thinking.* University of Chicago Press, Chicago.

Cross-cultural Perspectives

Note: The "Introduction" and the sections in this chapter on "Cross-cultural Studies", 1, 2 and 3 are, with minor revisions, taken from a previously published peer-reviewed article on the subject of groups and cross-cultural studies (see readings). All other sections are original and written for this book.

Introduction

Just about all of my work – therapeutic, training, organisational and academic – is cross-cultural, and in two languages, English and Swedish. I work with culturally homogenous groups of cultures other than my own, and with multicultural groups of up to 80 students from some 20 – 25 cultures, as well as in a variety of multinational companies around the world.

I have been aware for some time of the inadequacy of culture-bound group theories and models when dealing with such diverse groups. Group developmental models are invariably American in origin, certainly Anglo-Saxon in terminology, and increasingly seem to me to be so grounded in the cultural contexts of their origin that their applicability in a wider context is limited. When applied in the cultures of their origin, such models affirm, confirm and consolidate the cultural norms. When applied uncritically in multicultural groups, the result is a form of intellectual and normative colonialism.

As a result, I have been working on finding a less overtly culture-bound ground for exploring group evolutionary processes and the concomitant dynamics for a multicultural audience. And all the while fully aware that I can never be free from the influences of the accident of my birth into a family, a culture and a religion, my personal history – which includes 37 years residence in Sweden...so quite a paradox!

Let me start by establishing some working hypotheses around the construct of "culture", share some thoughts on existentialism and cultures, offer a revision of the constructs of culture and then proceed to link this to groups and groupwork.

Cross-cultural Studies, 1

A colleague of mine who researches in cross-cultural organizational issues has currently a collection of almost 400 definitions of "culture"! It is not my intention to explore the theme of culture as a study in itself other than in the context of this book and its theme. I will therefore attempt to keep such discussions open to "the informed and interested amateur", rather than the professional in the field. As such, my focus here is on culture at a national and/or ethnic level, sometimes bounded by a common language.

I define "culture" here as "recognisable and repeated patterns of behaviour internal to a bounded collection of people, and also externally between it and its environment". In other words, the behaviours we naturally use in our own cultural environments, and expect from co-cultural others, as well as the behaviours we collectively use in relation to other cultural environments. To a greater or lesser extent – itself culturally influenced – a person can exhibit similar patterns if behaving in another cultural environment than her own. To a greater or lesser extent, we are each of us representative of our original cultural environments. It is appropriate to say that the generalities of our culture probably influence us earlier and more than the specific peculiarities of our families, inasmuch as we are born onto families of people already embedded in their socio-cultural world.

I have chosen three dimensions or aspects of culture as being particularly relevant to the subject of groups. These form a continuum and are:

INDIVIDUALISM – FAMILISM – COLLECTIVISM.

Two of these – Individualism and Collectivism – are well-established constructs in cross-cultural studies. The third – Familism – was introduced by Annick Sjögren, a French ethnologist resident and researching in Sweden for many years; it is also used by Marin, a researcher into Hispanics in the USA, though named "Familialism" in his study.

I will add two sub-constructs, the first acknowledged in the research, the second more fully intuitive: the sub-construct of Familism and Collectivism, which I call "Embedded Familism", that is, Familism embedded in a Collective; and "Bounded Individualism", that is Individualism bounded by the family.

Here is a brief description of core issues for each, with suggestions for illustrative examples taken from the literature (with the exception of "Bounded Individualism", where intuition and experience are my sources). A dilemma with examples is that they both delimit and exclude, so please view all examples as guidelines to exemplify the issues– even if somewhat stereotypically - rather than absolute statements of fact. Please feel free to add and subtract from your own knowledge and experience.

INDIVIDUALISM: Identity is self-defined, also interpersonally defined. Membership of any sort is largely voluntary, and often strategically chosen by individuals for their own purposes. (USA, Australia, UK, Northern Europe)

FAMILISM: Identity is defined by family-membership, family status, sibling position and responsibilities. Other memberships are usually in the context of the extended family. (The Jewish Tradition; Mediterranean/Latin Europe; Catholic, Orthodox and Islamic cultures)

COLLECTIVISM: Identity is in group membership, which becomes a "given". Group is embedded in the larger social collective. (Japan, Korea)

EMBEDDED FAMILISM: The family is embedded in other social structures, for example clan, tribe, ethnic group, class group, which are in turn, embedded in the collective of an ethnic group in a defined geographical area. (Sub-Saharan Africa, China, Arabic and Islamic cultures)

BOUNDED INDIVIDUALISM: Identity is in family membership etc, with some latitude to individually explore the environment. (Ireland, Israel in my personal experience. Probably also the Mediterranean as a socio-cultural region).

As macro-level constructs, these nevertheless provide a solid ground for distinctions in cross-cultural attitudes and behaviours in groups. It is immediately noticeable that the "Group and Team" industry, both theoretically and through countless training-programs, originates in Individualistic cultures. In my experience of working multiculturally, people from Embedded Familistic and Collectivistic cultures have little or no need for training in group-membership and leadership along Individualistic lines. They behave in cultures where so much about groups is "given" and accepted as the cultural norm. Personal sub-optimisation in a group setting is also normal, rather than an individual choice in a strategic context as it can be in more Individualistic cultures. In consequence, models of group development and dynamics, grounded in one cultural context, may not necessarily be equally valid in others. This is certainly my experience. For example, working with a multicultural student group, the variety of reactions and competencies displayed when students are assigned project groups is fascinating – and culturally congruent. Any attempt to apply Western developmental and leadership models fails dismally – and believe me, I have tried them all! As a result, I now work from the above constructs, and find that most students are able to relate to them.

Some examples of multi-cultural groupwork within these frameworks:

Vignette 3, Multicultural/South West African:

1) I am working on a faculty team with a large multi-cultural group, with self-selected Process Groups. (The whole self-selection process is itself an example of cross-cultural issues). I am facilitating a Process Group during its first two meetings. At the end of the second sessions, a Ghanaian man says: "This group is my family here, you are all my cousins". He had otherwise been silent though attentive. This latter behaviour fits well with the description of an "intelligent person" amongst the Yoruba, another West African tribe as reported in Durojaiye: "First, there is the admiration

for the individual who does more listening than talking...(who) is believed to be taking in the issues under discussion...(this) wise person listens patiently and speaks only when all views...have been expressed. Second, there is the respect...given to the person who...can respond by placing the issue in its proper cultural context".

(I know and respect many groupwork colleagues who would have intervened around this man's silence – as seen from the perspective of Individualism).

Vignette 4, Multicultural/Latin

2) I am working with a multi-cultural student group, including a number of Italians. Whenever any of these Italian students asks a question, it is generally either the eldest male (considered and respectful questions), the female from the highest-status family (intellectually challenging questions), or the youngest (playful, light-hearted questions). The same applies to Mexican, Spanish and Latin American students. These also ask questions on each others' behalf, typical of Familism.

Vignette 5, Multicultural

3) I am working with multi-cultural Process Groups, where the opening format is to elicit statements beginning with "I want" and "We need". This is in order to raise awareness around individual and group issues. For North Americans and Northern Europeans, the "I

want" comes easy, and the "We need" is either a variation on "I want" or alternatively, a cognitive statement reflecting the individual's knowledge of group development models. For Africans and Asians, the "We need" statement often comes first, and the "I want" statement is a reinforcement of it. This confirms the research referenced in Triandis:" - we asked various samples of individuals in different parts of the world to complete 20 sentences that start with "I am..." we found that in collectivist cultures many of the sentence completions implied a group. For example, "I am a son" clearly reflects family; "I am a Roman Catholic" clearly reflects religion (group).

On the other hand, such statements were rare in individualistic cultures (where) people referred mostly to personal traits and conditions, e.g. "I am kind" or "I am tired". If we take the percent of group-related answers obtained from Illinois students as the basis, we found students of Chinese or Japanese background in Hawaii giving twice as many group-related responses and students in the Peoples' Republic of China giving three times as many such responses". (Again, imagine the impact of any intervention with only an Individualistic focus. My own work in such a group raises awareness around the two perspectives – the individual and the group – which may support mutual respect).

Cross-cultural Studies, 2

Edward Hall introduced the concept of "high context" and "low context" cultures, specifically in relation to communication. By "high context" he means cultures where most of the meaning of a communication is in the cultural context – the participants respond to a shared meaning-making. In "low context" cultures, each speaker needs to be explicit about the intended meaning of a communication. This is highly relevant to group facilitation in any homogenous or heterogeneous cultural setting.
The usual examples are:

HIGH CONTEXT	LOW CONTEXT
China	Switzerland
Japan	Germany
Korea	North America
Latin America	
Mediterranean	

In other words, working with homogenous groups from a high context culture other than our own, we as facilitators can expect that much of what is happening is beyond our comprehension. This certainly reflects my experience in Italy, and more so Finland. A favourite moment with a multi-cultural group in Italy was when, with the assistance of the Italians, we arrived at 15 ways of saying "yes" ("si"), only one of which actually meant "yes" in a sense that North Americans or Northern Europeans could recognise! The Italians had no difficulties distinguishing between them – we others were regularly perplexed. Another favourite was the occasion I worked myself to a standstill for two days with a group of silent Finnish managers, which ended with the CEO saying that their sessions with me had been "okay" – about the highest praise possible from a group of Finns.

And the opposite: I am working with a group in the USA, and at one point express that I feel uncomfortable with the focus on Political Correctness. I am immediately asked to clarify with what exactly I am uncomfortable – with examples – and whether my level of discomfort is such that I need some breathing space before we continue...

We need to be mindful that so much of group theory and methodology, in its American origin and development, is grounded in a low context culture, where being explicit is the cultural norm. Let us not apply this as a universal norm.

Cross-cultural Studies, 3

In my cross-cultural teaching, I often use Kurt Lewin's model of a distinction between Americans and

Germans, focused on the individual's boundaries between the private and the public. This is illustrated by a simple metaphor: if Americans and Germans were avocadoes, then the Americans would have a lot of permeable flesh around a small, hard and almost impermeable kernel. The Germans would have a smaller amount of permeable flesh, and a larger kernel. Lewin's point was the distinction between the boundaries of public and private between the two cultures. The construct "boundaries" here can be usefully replaced by "interactive interface".

More recently, Shamir and Melnick proposed "Boundary Permeability as a Cultural Dimension", referring in their article to Lewin's work. They distinguish between permeable and rigid boundaries (or "interactive interfaces"), and relate their model to the seminal cross-cultural studies currently available (see Recommended Reading). Taking the essential cultural dimensions from each of these authors' models, they apply their boundary concept ("permeable" versus "rigid") to each end of the dimensional continua.

They find there is a sufficient match to be able to support their proposal. In other words, they present a model of cultures based on boundary issues in relation to the environment, the environment being that which can be experienced as other than the culture itself. That is, a recognisable collective pattern of behaviour in relation to the culturally "other". To clarify and exemplify this point, let me return to the cross-cultural model I presented earlier, and add the boundary dimension. The slash (/) represents the interactive interface or boundary:

- Individualism: person/environment.
- Familism: person/family; family/kith and kin; kith and kin/socio-cultural environment.
- Collectivism: person/group; group/other groups; group/socio-cultural environment.
- Embedded Familism/person/family; family/clan; clan/ethnic group; ethnic group/environment.
- Bounded Individualism/person/family; person/environment

A further aspect is that, in the case of Familism, Collectivism and Embedded Familism, the person generally represents most or all of the other interfaces in that person's boundary with any environment. For example, family honour, clan loyalty, ethnic tradition. I recently experienced an expression of this: I was working in Toronto, and was wearing a recent present from a Ghanaian colleague of a woven scarf with his tribal motif on it. Later in the week, a taxi pulled up before me and the driver jumped out and greeted me joyously. He recognised the motif, was from the same tribe, and simply wanted to meet me. When he heard that my colleague was nearby, he dropped everything in order to meet him. I felt that I had been greeted by and was meeting the whole tribe.

Cultures and Existentialism

Having previously given existentialism a central place in the opening pages of this book, and now included a considerable section on culture, I feel a need to place them in the context both of each other and therefore of the whole.

Existentialism as a distinct philosophy of life is a predominantly Western notion, largely confined to Continental Europe and the United States. Existentialism is supported by a humanism most at home in Judaism and atheism; at the same time, the theistic existentialists – Kierkegaard, Buber, Marcel, Tillich and Jaspers, for example – are all convinced of the individual's freedom to choose to believe in the existence of God. Their existentialism consists largely of this element of, and responsibility for, choosing God – or not. The atheistic existentialists – Nietzsche, Sartre, Camus, de Beauvoir, Merleau-Ponty, for example – are engrossed by the responsibility to choose a meaning for our lives in the sure certainty that our impending and expected deaths make such an enterprise somewhat absurd. It is precisely that absurdity which is the nature of our human existence.

American existentialism, on the other hand, is distinguished by its optimism. Whilst most often associated with such figures as Rollo May and Irvin Yalom, American existentialism has its roots in the thinking of Abraham Maslow, who was a research assistant to the German neuro-surgeon Kurt Goldstein on his arrival in the USA during the 1930s. Goldstein's holistic thinking associates him more with Gestalt Psychologists like Wertheimer, Koffka, Köhler and even Lewin than other medical scientists. (Maslow was a great admirer of Wertheimer, whom he used as an example of "self-realisation", along with the anthropologist Ruth Benedict). It was Goldstein who first documented the brain's amazing ability to heal itself from injury by compensating for damaged parts with the wholeness of the brain – and indeed, the human organism – working to find its optimal expression in whatever circumstances.

Maslow took Goldstein's biological model and transferred it to the domain of human psychology and even philosophy with his famous "Hierarchy of Needs", where initial biological/physiological needs give way to self-realisation at the pinnacle: becoming the best we can be no matter what the starting-point or circumstances. Unintentionally, Maslow had started the "Peak Experience" industry, with its value-judgements on human experience. He had also laid the foundation for a less death-focused existentialism than the European version. In consequence, American existentialism has more room for terms such as "growth", "development", "possibilities" and "courage" in contrast with Continental Europe's love for

Kierkegaard's "angst" and the black-clad bohemians of Paris in the 1950s and 1960s.

At the same time, socio-cultural populations influenced by Christianity and Islam have an underlying belief in a life after death. (So have Orthodox Jews – when the Messiah has come, which, as yet, has not happened as they see it). Clearly, a life after death takes away some of the anxiety so beloved of existentialists – with the exception of those who see God as a choice as much as a given, and thus face themselves with the "angst" of their choice and its consequences.

Asia is generally dominated by Buddhism and Hinduism, both of which share a belief in re-incarnation. Re-incarnation as a fact of life and death has an impact on anxiety for the present and future incarnations, an impact which I can only imagine. I am a product of a Catholic upbringing and a later withdrawal from the Church and its teachings – though not necessarily from my theism - somewhere, somewhere, I still believe in God and so occasionally attend Catholic mass and take communion. So I still hold a somewhat diluted belief in a next life elsewhere– and this complicates my ability to even imagine a re-incarnated life back here again.

I have much less difficulty with the presence of my dead ancestors in my life, as is typical for the complexity of beliefs represented by China, or my connection to the whole of nature as would be typical of the traditional pantheism of sub-Saharan Africa, and the poetry of John Donne and William Wordsworth and their contemporaries. Much of Western "New Age" spirituality may also belong here.

And so to the "bottom line": where simple existence is concerned – being alive and here - I share its possibilities and limitations, its promise or its absurdity, with every other human being. While our socio-cultural settings and religious/philosophical beliefs may support our differentiation from each other, our mere existence unites us. I, like you, was born. We are both alive – well I was anyway when I first typed this line (Sunday, July 31, 2011). We will die, and we both know we will die. We know this both of ourselves and of each other. We may have various notions of what may or may not happen afterwards...but that is then and not now. Right now it is our existence as human beings which unites us.

One of the consequences here is that I have found myself moving away from a cross-cultural perspective (which focuses on reconciling differences) to a more multi-cultural one (which recognises and respects our distinctions as learned socialisation rather than intrinsic differences).

Existentially, you and I have more in common than we may have thought. We are, along with everyone else in the world, faced with the dilemma of how connected or separate we need to, want to and/or can be. I have earlier named this "The Existential Dilemma": the availability to us at every moment of a continuum from "Apart From Others" to "A Part Of Others".

And this can be seen, of course, as a variation of the

INDIVIDUALISM – FAMILISM – COLLECTIVISM

continuum, where our socio-cultural ground may be directly influencing where on the continua we find ourselves as group members. This is also and chicken-and-egg situation: which came first? Are our cultural norms emergent from some shared resolutions of "The Existential Dilemma" over many thousands of years? Or are our socio-cultural norms the source of our dilemma?

So yes: existentially it is precisely ME as who I am in all my socio-cultural complexity who is meeting you and the various groups I meet and work with – so an awareness of what both unites and/or distinguishes me, you and those groups is the existential heart of the matter.

Cultures and Groups

All of which brings me to a humbling, challenging and exciting admission: drafting this book has helped me to finally discard as universally applicable all the established group development theories and models which I have used over many years. Looking back with hindsight, I can see how my practice has evolved itself free from such constraints and safety nets.

As a result, my intention here in this book is to proceed AS IF 70 years or so of Anglo-American theorising and cultural colonisation of groups and groupwork were no longer universally applicable. I am aware that this is a huge step for colleagues who have used these models, and who have found them relevant. I am aware that I have taken this step myself, and survived, as have the groups with which I have worked in the 15 years it has taken me to become Tuckman, FIRO and, more recently, Wheelan-free!

And as I sometimes say to my students, 1.6 billion Chinese can't be wrong, a culture with a recognisable history of some 4 thousand years and a Confucian social psychology since 600 BCE. Along with the re-emergence of the Eastern European cultures, increased access to and exchanges with Asian cultures and the Indian sub-continent, as well as the post-colonial tragedies in much of Africa, it is no longer possible to confine or even limit our understanding of groups and teams to the ethnocentric models of one region. We have a lot to learn from others – and an opportunity to more appropriately use our existing knowledge and experience than to simply add it to the colonial burden we impose on others. Living and working multi-culturally as I do, I have found that my Gestalt training, knowledge and experience have been an invaluable support both personally and professionally. What follows is what works for me – it may even work for others, in whole or in part.

I am therefore choosing to start afresh, having named, acknowledged and owned my own cultural heritage. I humbly and strongly suggest the reader considers also doing the same – naming, acknowledging and owning your own cultural heritage and its influence on you as a person and as a group member and groupwork practitioner in whatever functional role. I return to this theme below, under the heading The Imagined Group. I regard this awareness and acknowledgement as the essential first step into the delights, challenges and excitements of a multicultural working environment.

Implications for Practice

The implications for practice of the above sections are the core content of the remainder of this book.

References and Recommended Reading:

Hall, Edward T., (1976). *Beyond Culture.* Doubleday. New York.

Harris, Phillip R., & Moran, Robert T. (1979). *Managing Cultural Differences.* Gulf Publishing Company. Houston, Texas, USA.

Hofstede, Geert. (1984). *Culture's Consequences.* Sage Publications. New York.

Marks, Robert B. (2002). *The Origins of the Modern World.* Bowman & Littlefield. New York.

Shamir B & Melnik Y (2002). *Boundary Permeability as a Cultural Dimension.* International Journal of Cross-cultural Management, vol. 2/2

Skromme Granrose, C & Oskamp S. (1997). *Cross-cultural Work Groups.* Sage Publications. Thousand Oaks, California.

PART 2 Defining Some Particulars

Introductory Guidelines and Terminology

Little or nothing in Part 1 is particularly controversial or new, even if one or another of my extrapolations of Lewin can occasionally raise an eyebrow. Some practitioners may find my discarding of standard models of group "development" to be challenging since I have not as yet offered an alternative. These introductory guidelines are meant as a theoretical and methodological support to my proposed alternative.

As indicated earlier, I will be using a number of constructs specific to my proposal, such as group evolution (as change over time) and the notion of a field emergent group at least analogous to the established psychological construct of the personal self as emergent of the social field, a natural part of our being-in-the-world.

The group is a living organism interacting with and within its physical environment as well as a social psychological entity interacting philosophically and psychologically (that is, emotionally and cognitively) with its environmental others as a collective. These interactions are both individually initiated through each member, and collectively as an entity. As an entity, a group may interact with another group – another department, for example, in an organizational setting, or the designated leader, or manager or facilitator who, while certainly of the field of the group/leader whole, is not a member of the group on an equal standing with other members.

Socio-cultural norms and expectations will also be at work, defining the parameters of acceptable behaviours and the possibilities for deviations. In groups of more than one culture, these parameters are likely to be central to the interpersonal and sub-group dynamics of interaction. Historical and political connections are also part of this perspective: a mixed group of Irish and English, or Germans and Jews, or Russians and Latvians for example will have issues that may be more symbolic than actual, though certainly influencing perceptions and interactions. I well remember my own physical discomfort with the accents and idioms of middle to upper-class English people where I was a minority of one from the working class of the Republic of Ireland. The individual people disappeared into an ugly mass I angrily named "you fucking Brits".

What I am attempting here is to find a set of core concepts and methodologies which will support me – as a group leader/facilitator - to meet each group in its uniqueness and allow its natural evolution. I also want to relate these ideas and practices to people performing tasks, as formally organized work-groups or teams, where the socio-relational aspects of working with groups meets the functional role demands of task and performance. This is the main theme of Chapter 7.

I then move to explicating aspects of groupwork which have long fascinated me – a sense of relating to more than one entity at one and the same time. This will often be expressed by group members behaving in ways that seem curiously inconsistent, as if they were here and elsewhere at the same time. This is the main theme of Chapter 8.

But first, a distinction I find useful:

Group Process and Group Dynamics

I will begin here by distinguishing between Group Process and Group Dynamics by assigning each a distinct meaning in the context of my thinking. (and yes – this is yet another AS IF!).

For me, Group Process is a term for the evolution or change over time which occurs in any gathering of people connected somehow in space and time: a bus queue at a bus stop over the time between buses; a group of students in a classroom over the period of a term or a school year; a personal development group meeting weekly over a prescribed number of sessions; a project group in an organization over the life of the project. Incidentally, "space" here includes cyberspace and the contemporary process of self-organizing and self-regulation amongst people who may never have met f2f, as the newspeak goes these days.

Models of the phases/stages of group development are attempts to capture the change over time of a group in its process. Whilst often far too ethnocentric to be as generalisable as they are used – see the Singapore example above – they do at least attest to a notion that a collection of strangers can become a social psychological entity - a self-defined group - over time.

Group Dynamics are the in-the-moment behavioral events which both support the Process and even express it. For example, the Dynamics involved in the resolution of interpersonal disagreements between the people in a group – accusations, defences, counter-accusations, side-taking, aggression, withdrawal etc. - may well lead to a period of relative stability in the change Process of the group as it moves from one state of stability to another through change. This new stability may be expressed through co-operative Dynamics between the group members, such as apologies, supportive statements, acknowledgements etc.

To summarise:

Group Dynamics: that which is happening, now, in the moment, between group members and sub-groups as well as between members, sub-groups and the group-as-a-whole and the formal leader/manager/facilitator. Group Dynamics are the interface events between one and another, including apparent non-events.

Group Process: that which occurs to the wholeness of these group members as a collective over time, both as the temporary outcomes of the preceding/ongoing dynamics AND the ground out of which the dynamics emerge, where that shifting ground is then the setting for the enactment of these dynamics. Together, the process and the dynamics form what is called (after Lewin) the situation of the group/facilitator whole, often the most figural context for group change, in the absence of traumatic events within or around the members/facilitator whole as a field.

These two constructs will be the frames for a further exploration of various kinds of groups, at a later stage below. But first, allow me to introduce some core concepts in my proposal for an alternative to standard approaches to groups.

Social Groups, Work-Groups and Teams: An Introduction

General Introduction

Those of my readers acquainted with Celtic mythology will know of the three-faced sculptures found in various parts of Ireland, and probably deriving from Hecate, the three-headed lady of Greek mythology. And those of you acquainted with Christianity will know of the Holy Trinity. So hardly a surprise that an Irish Christian like me would think in trios, as I do as I now move into introducing some core constructs for my model! First I will introduce what I call the "Babushka Trio" - the Social Group, the Work Group and the Team. These will be followed by another and more central trio: the Actual, Imagined and Emergent Group. But first an illustrative mini-case:

Vignette 6, Sweden

In order to set the scene for the main issues at stake here, allow me to open with a highly condensed summary of a recent facilitation job I did: I am asked by a Divisional Director of a Swedish Government agency to attend and facilitate a Management Team two-day retreat. The attendees are described as Department Heads meeting under the leadership of a Divisional Director. In opening the retreat, introducing me and the purpose of session, the Director shows a power-point diagram of the High Performance Team Index

(HPTI) as filled in and processed after their most recent monthly meeting, alongside the results of their meeting previous to that one. Clearly, the scores are on the way up. The Director is pleased and asks for comments. One person responds enthusiastically. No-one else joins in.

My curiosity is aroused and I ask if I may intervene. To cut a long story short, it transpires that the enthusiastic member is the Deputy Director – the only person currently present along with the Director who had attended the previous meeting. The remaining fourteen people had not been there. The same two plus one other of those now present had attended the meeting prior to that. Further conversations revealed that each department has a manager, an assistant manager and a substitute manager.

The Management Team in front of me was composed almost entirely of substitute managers, with a few assistant managers. The only Department Manager present was the Deputy Director. Clearly, the HPTI results of a meeting so few of those present had actually attended was of little or no relevance to anyone – except the Director, and the HR staff-member responsible for implementing HPTI as an organizational development (OD) intervention in such temporary work-groups.

The Director and HR were probably under a common management illusion: "if we call them a group" (or worse, as in this case - a "team"), "then that's what they are."

*****

Three Dimensions of Team

Partly because of the recent and current popularity of the construct "team", I am choosing to start there on this journey into group territory. I see a team as the ultimate expression of group life, a status or condition available to all groups, though experienced by very few. Becoming a team is not something that is "done to" a collection of people by someone external to that collection. Becoming a team happens or it doesn't, and is a process from within the field of the collective of the people involved. Not becoming a team is as important a message to the environment as is becoming one. And it happens over time. Three days running around a forest, crossing rivers and climbing trees is probably great fun, and certainly very expensive. It does NOT create a team that can function as such back in the workplace. Teams create themselves, from within, and over time.

Nevertheless, "teams" in the workplace and the use of "coaches", and "consultative competence" as an organizational intervention as well a management style have had a major impact on organizational life. An aspect of this is the use of various measurement instruments to tell a "team" what the members already know – namely, how they function as a collection of people either in a workplace and/or with an assigned or self-chosen task.

In order to explore this topic, allow me to use the metaphor of a Russian babushka doll, with dolls within dolls within dolls. If I take the outer and visible whole as a team – however abstract or idealized - then opening that will reveal the work-group inside. That is, a collection of people involved in various ways with performing tasks through work, whether individually or interactively, professionally or voluntarily.

And here is an important sub-categorisation of work group: there is the work group of a training course, educational group, supervision group for example, where the learning focus is individual and there is little or no shared product of the individual work.

Then there is an organizational work group – a department, say – where individual efforts and contributions are managed and combined to produce a collective result. And sometimes these may overlap as in the case of a department the members of which are on a training programme as a department, learning together to achieve a collective result.

I am calling both of these work groups, while acknowledging the distinctions between them: so, a work group with a focus on individual achievements, and a work group with a focus on a shared, collective outcome.

Opening the work group babushka will reveal the social group inside it, a collection of people as social human beings in their existential and socio-cultural context. In some cultures, I can open the social group doll and may reveal an individual, representing all the individuals involved. In other cultures, the family or even some other definable sub-group may be regarded as the smallest social unit in society.

Having opened here by moving from team to work-group to social group, I will now explore each in reverse order – social group, work-group and finally team. A distinctive feature of this approach is that both here and throughout this book, I will be moving back and forth between themes which are at times both embedded in each other and also possible to consider as discrete from each other. In other words, AS IF a team is a special form of work-group, and AS IF both a team and a work-group are always also a social group, and that these can be managed and/or facilitated differently. One of my many proposals is that teams and professional work-groups can sometimes benefit from being met as a social group, a gathering of human beings who incidentally happen to share a workplace and task. At other times, my focus may be entirely work, function and task related. Examples of each will be given where appropriate.

This is the skill of acknowledging the whole while simultaneously being free to meet its parts. And, of course, acknowledging the parts while simultaneously being free to meet the whole. I am well aware here that I am treating hypothetical constructs – social group, work group and team AS IF they were discrete parts of an established whole – the team babushka. I find it not only intellectually satisfying to do this, I also find it methodologically rich in possibilities. Finally, my practice has convinced me that I regularly meet a whole of which these three constructs can at any time be realizable as discrete parts, as integral aspects of that whole.

This for me is no different – though considerably more complex, of course – than meeting my best friend who is also a grandfather and a skilled psychotherapist. When I meet him with his grandchildren, I am fully aware that still as my friend he will occasionally choose to divert his attention away from me to the children and be in his organically acquired social role as grandfather. He is highly unlikely to be present either to them or to me in his chosen professional role as psychotherapist – and also that this role is also always present and available to him should it be required or appropriate.

As such, the whole is the gestalt of the parts, just as the whole gives meaning to each of its parts and how they are dynamically related.

Social Groups

I have found it increasingly useful to define any collection of three or more people as a Social Group. It is AS IF the Social Group is the core of any gathering of three or more people, whatever their purpose or task. Why three? Well, a lone individual is a person; two such persons is a dyad. A person and a dyad are sub-groups of a trio as a social group. In fact, it is precisely the availability to a trio of numerous combinations of persons and dyads which makes three the magical number for a preliminary definition of a group. The two people in a dyad are either together, with each as part of the dyad – or separate, with each apart from the other, at best a virtual dyad. The three people in a trio have a range of variations at their disposal.

With a trio, a number of social configurations are possible. A useful experiment here for the reader is to mark three pieces of paper A, B and C, and then move them around in all of the configurations possible. Imagine the possibilities if these were people: did A move voluntarily away from B and C, or was it B and C who moved away from A? Or was it B who moved away and C who followed? What might the impact on each of the three have been of that? Did B and C agree to voluntarily move away from A? What might the impact on A have been of that event?

Often, I will offer an opportunity to a group to psycho-physically gestalt these usually implicit dynamics by asking for three volunteers, and requesting them to configure themselves as a trio, silently, in as many variations as possible, all the while checking their awareness of the impact on them each time there is a movement. Remaining participants are invited to observe the dynamics of the movements and also check their reactions. This gives an opportunity to explore not only the social mechanics of sub-grouping, but also the psycho-emotional dynamics at play with each re-configuration.

Increase the number of papers/people to five, and observe and sense how the complexity grows exponentially. Try seven, and you'll maybe understand how impossible it is for any group member or observer (or manager, or facilitator) to keep track of the all of the possible relational and sub-group dynamics involved. The best we can hope to do is track the dynamics of sub-group formation as people connect and interact, and notice the patterns of sub-groups as the dynamics settle and the whole group temporarily stabilizes.

This is a reason for the use of five members being seen as ideal for a self-led team. From seven upwards, a group is becoming something closer to an organisation with a need for management and the parameters of structure.

And so to a more nuanced definition of a group: Three or more people who

1) Are defined by another/others as a group, and/or

2) Self-define, individually and collectively, as a group.

So a trainer who looks at a list of the names and occupations of workshop participants who have not yet met, may well decide that "this looks like a good group". And thus a group is created in the mind of the trainer, imaginary and projected though it may be. The same applies the moment a participant sees the same list before having met the others – this participant is already relating to these unknown others, and maybe even thinking of them all as "my" training group, and anticipating events in the light of past experience of group membership.

In this way also, a gathering of people at a bus-stop can be regarded as a group. As a social animal and being, each person has a capacity to relate to others in any number of ways and the wholeness of these interconnected relations self-organize and self-regulate the emergence of a social unit – a group. As such, this unit can respond to its physical and social situation in a mutually coherent way: a sudden heavy shower of rain, a half-empty bus not stopping, the arrival of a woman with a push-carriage, and a youngster on her hip: each of these will be responded to as much as a pattern of the wholeness of the people involved rather than simply as a disconnected series of individual actions.

The first example above is different in character to the second and third. With the first– the change in the weather – the Social Group probably remains as such, a gathering of people simply being with each other, though maybe now sharing umbrellas. The passing bus may evoke the use of mobile phones and complaints on behalf of all, so a type of functional role emerging. With the arrival of the woman with the two children, an element of probable shared task is also arriving. There may need to be some implicit or explicit recognitions of a move from only being together to being and doing together. In other words, the Social Group is now also a Work-Group with a common task which can include Functional Roles, such as, in this case, lifting the baby-carriage onto the bus, and allowing the mother on the bus before her "turn".

The Work-Group

I have used this mundane and simplified example above to bring attention to the two-dimensional nature of work-groups. They are at one and the same time, a Social Group of people being together and also a Functional Task Group, with a focus on doing work – either individually or together (see above). It is AS IF there is a Social Group of people embedded in a Work Group as members of the former take on or are assigned Functional Roles in order to perform a task in the latter.

The tensions between the needs of people in their social interactions and the demands of their functional roles which may include inter-functional interactions are at the core of organizational life, and yet, in my considerable experience, most managers behave as if their work-groups were one-dimensional Functional Task Groups, where the personal and social aspects are often seen as a hinder to something called "efficiency", rather than a necessary element which needs their care and attention every bit as much as the management of operations and tasks.

In addition, the models of stages or phases of group development which are most often in use in businesses and organizations focus exclusively on the development of the social group. Indeed, both Tuckmann (a "Performing" phase) and Wheelan (a "Work" phase), place these after the initial social phases. Whilst the other models will often be connected to the types of task most appropriate for any particular phase, there seems to be an assumption that the Social Group somehow disappears at some stage, never to re-appear in any influential way ever again. My proposal is that the Social Group is the most enduring and stable expression of individuals self-organising and self-regulating in order to create social wholes.

And yet, staff-members including managers come and go all the time and few Work-Groups remain stable over time in terms of membership. In other words, the core glue of the Social Group is continuously being dissolved and little social stability is available to the Functional Task Group, which is, after all, composed of the same people though in their functional roles. It is to a large extent this sense of shared stability as a social unit which creates the ground for part 2 of the definition above – "self-define, individually and collectively, as a group". This can be expressed by someone saying "we" when referring to the group, and no-one reacting with an objection as a discrete individual.

Such an ever-changing Work-Group can become so focused on establishing and maintaining sufficient social stability (whatever "sufficient" means for that particular social group) that the work task becomes secondary. In the case of the opening anecdote, it is very probable that this is the case. There is also such an absence of continuity of membership that a Social Group is unlikely to ever emerge other than arbitrarily and temporarily and without continuity – and it is my contention that such situations need the support of an experienced facilitator or manager with sound facilitator training. Equally unlikely is the formation of an integrated Functional Task Group in the face of the apparent irrelevance of HPTI scores to most people present. I would have some difficulty referring to this Divisional Management "Team" as a functioning Work-Group. It seemed at best to be a gathering of independent reporting functions with little if any active inter-functional connections, these functions merely reporting back on a number of discrete tasks apparently being implemented in an organisational vacuum.

The Work Group of the opening mini-case for this section needs to be met as such – an almost random collection of discrete functional tasks, working largely independently of each other. Regarding this collection as a Team, and judging and "measuring" it as such is, for me, utterly counter-productive from a management perspective. To begin with, the people here are being objectified as Functional Tasks only. Secondly, they are being objectified as a Team...I am certain that they were well aware of the absurdity of this designation along with the absurdity of the manager so designating them.

Teams

Which brings us to the interesting issue of Teams: what with "Hair-team", "Courier Team", "Service Team" and the plethora of proposed other teams around us, I am unsure of the value of attempting to restore some meaning to the term. And yet, with dogged determination, I am willing to try. Such is the value I attach to the very few teams worthy of the name that I have encountered.

I define a team as a work-group the members of which are aware of the presence of and distinctions between itself as a Social Group and itself as a

Functional Task Group (Work Group), and take care of itself as both. Such a team will know when to attend to its personal and social needs and relations, and when to attend to its functional and inter-functional interactions, and on how these influence each other.

Whilst a formal leader/manager function is usually necessary for a Work-Group, a Team is fine with rotating leadership from within itself, with members taking on or being internally assigned by a consensus of fellow members a leader function as appropriate. I return to this theme below.

This preliminary consideration of teams completes the three-dimensional aspect of groups in organizations – the Social Group, which together with Functional Task Roles forms the Work-Group, and the Team as a fully integrated purposeful whole of both of these, with self-responsibility. The Social Group, that is, people as social animals and philosophical and psychological beings, will always be the core.

Social Groups, Work-Groups and Teams: Part 2 – Exploring the Parts

The Social Group

The Group Process of any gathering of people in time and space, here called a Social Group, is the change over time through which they move from a random gathering of individuals to a self-organized and self-regulated entity which may self-define as a group – or not, as the case may be. This can be seen AS IF the people concerned are each and together dealing with "the existential dilemma" – the condition of being a part of a whole with others, or of being apart from a possible whole – that is, apart from the other members - on the margin psychologically/emotionally or even totally separated through physical absence.

The Dynamics are the behaviors and interpersonal relations which both create and then maintain a desired condition for each member, or for each member from the perspective of the others – being a part of or being apart from that particular collective. These are the dynamics of apparently individual or delimited interpersonal behaviors which, at the collective group-as-a-whole level of complexity, self-organize and self-regulate both the dynamics and the process of the Social Group.

From this perspective, there are in a group few if any discrete, individual behaviors in a vacuum. All behaviors are in the context of the other group members and the facilitator, and thus in relation to these environmental others as experienced by the person as member (Lewin's life space in action). In this way, any behaviour can be experienced as a dynamic expression in the moment of a collective group process over time.

How individuals relate to each other is also how the members of a social psychological entity called a group co-create the glue to hold itself together, or the water to allow separateness – or the exact and unique mixture of glue and water which THIS social group can accept, individually and collectively, and which creates the relational grist for the change mill over time of specifically THIS group.

The Work Group

I see a Work Group as essentially a Social Group with work tasks – either individual tasks as in a classroom, for example, or a shared task with individual assignments as in a commando unit.

Incidentally, I am not for a moment suggesting that my take on these events is the "right" or even "only" one available. It is, however, congruent with my approach, both theoretically and methodologically, and therefore that with which I am most at home, most secure – and precisely therefore, most open to challenge. This is where my trust in an inductive/deductive loop comes into play. Whilst my theory certainly informs my practice, it does not direct or constrain it. When something happens in my practice which questions my theory, then I change my theory...cold comfort, perhaps, for the reader! And yet, this is honestly how it is for me.

So: members of a work group in a commercial organization, for example, have a double identity – or anyway, a double identification. Some members are so willing to identify with their roles that their distinct identities as persons can seem to be diluted. Others keep their sense of personal identity to the fore – "who" I am comes always before "what" I am. And here is a classic cultural conundrum: in some cultures, I will be rewarded for being "authentically" "who" I am, and in others for being responsibly "what" I am, my functional role.

In cross-cultural terms, this is an aspect of the socio-cultural context in which we function. In the Industrialised West, it is possible to distinguish between the "who" and the "what" of me. In other cultures, such nuances are relatively meaningless. At the same time, in line with the existentialism of Sartre, for example, what I do is who I am...I am my actions, I am what I do in the moment...so a cross-cultural paradox: maybe the existentialists were less west-bank Parisian than they liked to imagine. I know from experience that when I do not over-invest in the differences between me and my experienced environment, then that environment has, as it were, an opportunity to respond in kind in the mutuality of our existential connection. In other words, when who I am – my actions in Sartre's view – is respectful of my perceived environmental other and honest though not pushy about myself.

Vignette 7, Ghana

A favourite and fairly recent example - I am working with a good friend and colleague in his home land of Ghana, with a training group of some 36 people. Two were white, and like me, European. Two others I knew to be non-Ghanaians. Now, my friend and I had worked our way into, through and out of a potentially divisive racist event many years previously and we had talked about the socio-cultural specifics of the tribal groups present in the room. We had talked about the importance of me including references to my family of origin as well as my son. I felt well-prepared. My friend opened the session, and handed over to me:

I greeted the group, stated that I would be brief and leave room for questions for areas of my life and work which may be of interest to them. So I did a brief presentation: who and what I am - my personal and professional background - my two sisters and my aunt in Dublin, my son in Sweden.

Out of nowhere: "You said we could follow our interest…you are Irish. Irish are usually Catholic. Are you?"

"Yes".

"Then as you certainly know, we are in Lent and in this week we have Ash Wednesday. A number of us are Catholics and have hired a bus to take us to mass. I'm sure we can find room for you. Okay?"

I agreed. My friend leaned towards me and whispered: "Ah! The Catholic tribe has come out of the closet and claimed you as their prize. Now even you are a tribal member!"

The dynamics here were those involved in a new person joining an existing system. The participant group had the same members as last time they had met. The faculty now had a new and temporary, guest member, who had in fact himself been trainer to five of the six of them. We were all of us about to spend a week of our time together in a residential facility.

My presence was a reminder of an external environmental other appearing at the boundary – the interface, where the dynamics occur and which the dynamics co-create. What happens at the interface is not the outcome of the intention of any of the parties to the engagement. It is rather the interplay of intentions, of responses and all the intricacies of such exchanges. There are certainly socio-cultural settings where the formalities of these social exchanges, for example, the status of age or family or class, will partly form the outcome.

The process involved how the participant group as a whole, the core faculty as a whole and the programme members as a whole – participants plus core faculty - moved from a previous stability through a change (my arrival and presence) towards and into a new stability, which encompassed my presence.

A sub-group – the Catholic "tribe" – had taken care of me. As part of a sub-group of the whole, I was now of course a part of the whole – as a person (The Social Group). In my functional role as facilitator of a training Work Group, I was free to function and be judged by my professional competence, not my incidental religious affiliation.

And all of this in the first ten minutes...the Social Group asserts itself, and the Work Group members can settle into their individual and sub-group learning.

Teams

A Team is a committed Work Group well aware and mindful of its co-existence as a Social Group, and a shared awareness of the interplay between the members as social-psychological, existential entities as well as Functional Roles. Whilst the members of a Work Group will maybe have some shared awareness that the combined efforts of individual members or sub-groups will have some relevance as a whole, the responsibility for seeing, planning and managing this cumulative effect is hierarchically above them. Their task efforts, individually and cumulatively, are in the hands of someone external to the Work Group, usually a formally appointed and mandated manager.

For a Team, all tasks are shared. The responsibility is a collective one, "ours" rather than "mine" and "yours". There are no discrete tasks which happen incidentally to be connected in some way to others. Each and all take responsibility for the performance of each and all – not only functionally in relation to the assigned task, but also socially in relation to each other.

A Team can make a consensus judgement about its competence and ability to take on and conclude a task. It can agree on what further training and development it may need for its members, or what externally sourced resources it may need – and take agreed steps to acquire such resources.

I have purposely used the singular impersonal pronoun "it" here to emphasise that a team emerges from a collection of persons as a psychological entity, a distinct unit, an "it" rather than a "they", a "we" which is a true description rather than some politically correct pretense.

Included here is an awareness of when the members may be too close to events, so that calling in an external resource such as a facilitator is always an option. A Team is also mindful of and sensitive to its impending death and the uselessness of fighting against it. In consequence, one of the characteristics of a team is knowing when to disband and allow the members to further develop themselves elsewhere as they bring with them their unique experience of having been a team-member. A Team will know when to celebrate its achievements, and also when to mourn its own passing as a shared sense of an approaching "sell by" date becomes acknowledged.

A Team forced to function as if it still were such beyond its own sensed "sell by" date becomes professionally incompetent and personally limiting. When naturally rotating leadership, in the context of the task and intentions, is replaced by a member or formal manager assuming a managerial role "in order to keep the team going", then bye-bye team. Teams are not managed. They are supported in their self-development and challenges by competent OD consultants and are intrinsically self-led.

A Team is a Work Group which can accept and appreciate the value of its interpersonal relatedness in expressions of itself as a Social Group – and then get back to work with a focus on the external task, having just accomplished much with its internal possibility of becoming a self-defined group. If you have ever belonged to a Team, for however short a time, you will know what I am talking about.

***

I would like here to add another perspective on the same themes and to attempt a preliminary integration as a form of summary: I call this perspective Levels of Complexity.

By levels of complexity I mean the distinction between how the group setting and group events may be experienced by its members, and also perceived by a non-member, such as a facilitator. (Levels of complexity have been addressed in group literature as "Levels of System", a construct I find to be misleading).

In a Social Group, the basic level is that of the person and the uniqueness of each Personal sense of self and also the uniqueness of how each of us can experience what may appear to be the shared events of group life. Each group member brings herself in all her complexity to the group and is distinguishable in her uniqueness from all others.

The Personal becomes very quickly subsumed in the Interpersonal, that is, all situations between a person and others, whether one-to-one or one-to-some. Such situations are, by their very nature, unpredictable, spontaneously creative events of relationship-building, with no guaranteed outcome, whatever the goal. And these need not be aware, conscious acts of agency.

Silent agreement or disagreement with the actions or words of another member are, for me, examples of the interpersonal which will sooner or later be expressed in words or deeds, directly or indirectly.

The next level of complexity is that of the sub-group, or part of the whole. A sub-group can be formal or informal. The formal is known, visible, obvious – gender, ethnicity, profession for example. The informal are those which emerge and find form during the life of the Social Group and are generally relational in nature, including a sub-group of one whether by the choice of that person in relation to all the others, or of the others to her. They can consist of members who discover common interests, for example, or simply feel socially attracted to each other. Informal sub-groups can often be a bridge between their formal versions, for example, when the informal contains a mix of genders or ethnicities.

Most complex is The Group-As-A-Whole, that which is different than the sum of its parts (members), that unique collective that is THIS group and no other, a matrix of relationships that shifts and changes over time.

Finally, society itself and all of the social contexts each member lives in and brings with them to group meetings is the complex setting of group events.

To summarize:

Levels of Complexity

- Social Group
- The Socio-Cultural Setting
- Group-As-A-Whole
- Sub-Group (Formal/Informal)
- Interpersonal
- Personal

Figure1

Work-Groups

Turning now to the Work-Group, where functional task roles are the distinguishing characteristic, we begin with Functional, a manager say, and then Interfunctional of course: a manager – subordinate interaction for example. Functional Sub-Groups in an organizational setting will always be primarily formal, though it is here that the interplay between the Social Group and the Work-Group can often lead to the emergence of informal functional sub-groups. These are generally invisible, especially to management, and can often take on a life of their own (see below, Working at the Interface, this chapter). In an organization, the Functional Group-As-A Whole, such as a project group or department, is itself a sub-group of a larger whole – a division, for example – just as each are sub-groups of the organization as a whole. The larger whole influences its parts, just as the parts may also influence both other parts as well as the larger whole. In addition, we may need to take into account the reactions of the parts and/or the whole to any influence – is it accepted, rejected, ignored, given lip-service?

Here is a visual summary of the connections between the Social Group and the Work-Group, with the Team as the self-led integration of both.

Levels of Complexity

Social Group	Work Group	Team
	Socio-cultural surroundings	
Socio-cultural surroundings	Organisation	Both
Group as a Whole	Functional Group as a Whole	Both
Sub-group (Formal/Informal)	Functional Sub-Group	Both
Interpersonal	Inter-functional	Both
Personal	Functional	Both

Figure 2.

Working at the Interface

In my experience, most organizational development or dynamics (OD) work is at the interface of the personal and the functional, that is between people as people and the same people as task-focused roles in a functional work context. Even when the presented issue is of tensions between a sub-group and another, or a sub-group and a larger whole which includes it, the attitudes expressed are likely to be a complex mix of the personal and the functional.

On the most basic level, the personal can take over from the functional in the case of an alcoholic manager, for example, whose personnel cover up for her functional incompetence and thus support her continued drinking.

The opposite would be the hyper-rational manager who refuses to take into account that a subordinate is still mourning a dead parent on the grounds that "she should be over it by now – we pay people to do their jobs, not mope around the workplace all day".

Vignette 8, Sweden

A favorite of mine in terms of the dynamic complexity of the relational and functional interacting with each other is a special project group set up in a normally rather bureaucratic organization under a dynamic, entrepreneurial leader. I was in as trainer with this group on a number of occasions, and witnessed how it took off and made waves. The project was judged to be so successful that the leader was promoted elsewhere in the organization. For some months, no replacement was found or assigned. The project group became not only leaderless, but also rudderless. A number of members returned quietly to their former positions. Those that remained became a highly informal functional sub-group, selecting training opportunities and using the project budget to fund further training. I noticed that I was meeting a core sub-group in various training events in other parts of the company. By the time a new manager was appointed, there was no project group remaining – though one of the most highly trained core sub-groups imaginable. Of the five members of the core, three are currently in senior executive positions in the original organization and still form a powerful and influential network. Quite simply, they became a self-led, high achieving team, and I am happy to have been involved in their evolution as such. And also to have been engaged by two of them as OD consultant to them and their current personnel, including former members of the original project group.

Implications for Practice

This overview is intended as a reiteration of a central theme: that groups, work-groups and teams can be viewed and worked with as both distinct from each other as well as usually inextricably linked and that we who work with these need to be able to grasp the whole while acknowledging the parts. We need to find a way to move between them appropriately, that is, within the context of our contracted task. My proposal is that much of our work, whether as managers, facilitators or OD consultants will be at the interface between these three dimensions. What follows throughout the remainder of this book is an examination of various aspects of this work.

Vignette 9, Sweden

In the meantime, an example of such interface work may support understanding: I am leading a training group in the move from therapist or manager into being an OD consultant. In other words, all participants are professionals looking to expand or change their areas of competence. As anyone who works with groups knows, there is always something going on in groups – and this one is residential, we are together 24 hours a day, so plenty of time for issues to emerge. In other words, both in terms of group dynamics and group process.

While it is tempting – believe me, I know - to set aside some scheduled "process time" when working with educational and training groups, I have found this to be counter-productive in general and absolutely self-defeating in the context of a training program exploring OD work in theory and practice. Such a practice sends a message that process is somehow separate from everything else, whilst it is my contention that group process and dynamics are forever present. I am content to run the programme as a mix of experiential and didactic sessions, and to allow the "goings on" to emerge and be facilitated as they emerge.

On an afternoon in Module 2 of three of this training programme, whatever exercise I suggest is chatted about, performed casually, and then dropped. Eventually, a silence occurs.

I distinguish between "restful" and "restless" silences. In a restful silence, I feel and am relaxed and patient. In a restless silence, I can feel, sense, intuit that there is more action in the air, maybe looking for a direction, or maybe an approving nudge from me as facilitator.

This silence was, for me, restful. I said a few words about restful and restless silences, including my sense of this having been a restful one, signaling the end of a piece of work in the group. We closed the day's session.

The following morning, I suggested an "Open House". This is NOT a round in the conventional sense. It is an open session, where anyone may or may not say anything, and where everyone is free to respond, question and comment. It transpired during this that the group had had a fantastic post-dinner session after I had gone to bed, where they played a feedback game with each other. Each and all were enthusiastic about the game and its value to them, individually and as a group, and how different they felt in each other's company THIS morning, compared to earlier mornings.

From the perspective presented here, I would suggest that a Work Group with an Individual Goal Focus, typical of a training or educational group, had played with the self-organising needs of itself also as a Social Group, and come out available for more individual work together.

I honestly do not believe that a scheduled "Feed-Back Session" could ever be timed with the perfection of this group's timing: they held off my suggestions of work, closed the program work session which was related to me, and then continued with the inner work of the social group in its own time – thus allowing the working group to focus on work again and continue. My task here was to privately acknowledge my frustration and irritation as my every intervention seemed to evaporate before it landed, bracket my sensations and turn my curiosity to following the dynamics as they played themselves out and the process settled. This is the joy of field attunement...to follow rather than to lead, to always be learning rather than always knowing in advance.

And then to share my learning with the group with which it had been co-created, as I did with the professional development training group mentioned in the above vignette.

Another Trio of Groups in the Room

Introduction

This Chapter is my attempt to describe and explain what has become the heart of the matter for me in my group-work over recent years as expressed and enacted in my practice. That practice has increasingly informed my thinking, and thus also my proposal here for a theory, methodology and practice for groups in our increasingly diverse socio-cultural environments, where the values, customs and norms of any one sub-group is not intrinsically more valid or valuable than any other, apart from any actual or perceived power differentials which may be in play as forces of the field concerned.

And I repeat: this approach is not based on some idealized notion of society. It is rather firmly grounded in my experiences, reflections, readings and learnings over a busy life as an international wanderer and Jack-of-Many-Trades. The cognitive base is in the preceding pages: existentialism, field theory, Gestalt psychology and therapy, multiculturalism, group dynamics and group process.

And most fascinatingly – for me, anyway – is that what follows in this Chapter is so new to me in terms of description and explication (though not practice!), that I struggled to find a text that I found acceptable as an expression of what I wanted to communicate. Some of that struggle is probably still evident...

These constructs have taken a long though usually straight path from my attempts in the 1990s to free myself (and my students, and group clients) from the linear and sequential constraints of mainstream and ethnocentric group models. The path, while straight, became increasingly challenging in all its apparent simplicity. The challenge became firstly, to find the language and concepts that would describe and explain this path; and secondly, to package it in a manner that was relevant and useful for others. Whilst it is certainly reasonable to believe, with Lewin, that there are few things as practical as a good theory – it is a fact that there are few things as useless as a theory no one understands or that no one finds attractive and potentially useful enough to even attempt to understand.

So my hope is that this core element in my proposal for a valid alternative to mainstream models is finally ready to go into print.

Allow me to open with a metaphor to support your understanding of my new trio of metaphors: I used to travel "home" to Dublin from England with my Swedish wife and son, my new family. Within a few minutes, I was a son to my father and to my mother (two very different sons, I assure you) and a big brother to my two younger sisters (again, two very different big brothers). Again, within minutes, my parents are now parents-in-law and grandparents, my sisters now sisters-in-law and aunties. We have each and all of us moved seamlessly into a complexity of life-spaces, of behavioural situations, each and all more or less congruent with each other.

For example, my natural big-brother banter with my sisters sounds – I later learn – as conflictual to my wife. She believes we are arguing. And so on. We are each and all of us behaving in a number of phenomenal situations, or life-spaces, AS IF they were simultaneously available and mutually valid. Another example: I am extremely sensitive to the degrees of drunkenness of my alcoholic father, so I judge his antics with my son within that "original family" frame. My wife is aghast – my "new family" frame. I am caught between the two. I say "two" – though the multiplicity of behavioural situations creates a dynamic beyond my or our or anyone's capacity to track and manage.

If I behave in the context of my wife and our son, then I am likely to offend my father. My mother, sisters and I know all too well where that can lead, Christmas Day or not. Anyway, I trust you will have accepted the relevance of the metaphor. As social beings, we are often dealing with a multiplicity of life-spaces. Clearly, this is something we bring with us to the groups in and with which we work. My simplification here is to frame this within three simultaneously occurring social contexts – the Actual, Imagined and Emergent Group.

The Actual Group

The Actual Group is that specific collection of persons present at any given time in the life of that collective. So, those I call Adam, Birgitta, Charles, Denise, Eric etc., in alphabetical order, the actual people gathered in the same space at the same time.

The Imagined Group

Adam, Birgitta, Charlie, Denise, Eric and company each bring with them previous group experiences, various "shoulds" and "musts" for themselves, other group members and the facilitator. Combined, these create a sort of virtual group as imagined by the participants, a kind of standard or preferred or known mould with which this actual group and facilitator is about to be compared and judged by each and all concerned. This is, of course, perfectly normal. We all use our previous experience as a reference point in a new situation. Some of us tend to stay longer with the old mould - or indeed moulds - than others. The constraints or flexibilities of our socio-cultural values, norms and concomitant behaviors play themselves out in this situation.

At the same time, other events are happening. On joining a group, I have proposed that a person needs to find a place on the A Part Of – Apart From continuum of what I have called the Existential Dilemma. Some will tend towards one or other end of this continuum, or a balancing act around the middle – wherever that ever-shifting point turns out to be, at any given moment.

Vignette 10, Sweden

An example: Adam arrived late for the first of three Thursday lunch- Sunday lunch residentials, reluctantly made a minimal introduction of himself, and kept to himself during breaks. He then declared later during this first module of a program on personal and professional development that he had no interest in endless, chitchat process debriefings or particularly in small-group work – he would only promise to attend focused process sessions, theory and application sessions (negotiated membership – even if somewhat unilateral). Another person voiced an opinion about how "we" as group members "should" behave. Yet another spoke to freedom of choice, as long as it doesn't affect "us" and the program. The remaining 9 people were silent, some looking towards me. I suggested an experiment, and described it as I designed it in my head. No one protested, and no-one showed much enthusiasm. So I continued. I asked the three who had spoken to seat themselves in different corners of the room, briefly repeating their words. The fourth corner was for "Don't know/mind". I asked the "speakers" to repeat their perspectives, and invited the others to join the corner they felt most agreement with. I then invited people to speak for their perspective from each corner, and suggested that everyone was free to move freely as the spirit moved them. Some took up positions between two corners. Some changed opinion from one corner to another. By the end, Adam had been joined by two others – one who admired and lacked his courage, one who supported him in principle, and felt strongly about it. From the perspective being presented here, the group had now explored how the Apart From – A Part Of continuum was being played out in the moment, with all its nuances. Adam found himself – and was seen to be - a member of a sub-group. The Actual Group now had a greater awareness of a central group issue – being "a part of" AND "apart from" - at group level, rather than at an individual/interpersonal level (Adam versus the rest of the group). (I can't help reflecting to what extent scapegoating in groups would be lessened if such sub-group dynamics received more focus).

A number of "Imagined Groups" had been enacted and explored, and Adam now had an actual group to respond to rather than only the imagined one he had brought with him. The same can be said of the others.

*****

Obviously, cross-cultural aspects will play a part here. Whatever the ground of, or awareness around, the tendency towards a place on the continuum of the existential dilemma, it is likely that much of the actual group's life will be taken up with this question over time. Language plays a part here in highlighting the issue: the ease of use of "We" or "I" can give the facilitator an idea of the dynamics involved. Incidentally, insisting for example on the use of "I" statements as many of my Gestalt colleagues can do is counter-productive from the perspective of my proposal, as it un-necessarily interferes with the organic dynamics and process of the group, especially in cross-cultural or multicultural contexts.

In my experience, the stronger the socio-cultural norms, the more likely a culturally homogenous group is to deal with the presence of these norms as "shoulds" and "musts", and thus influence the dynamics and process in order to preserve the socio-cultural status quo.

A multicultural group – even of two cultures – will be faced with the possible differences between the socio-cultural "shoulds" and "musts", and the challenge of finding a mutually acceptable or at least tolerable compromise – or not.

As facilitator, I am clearly involved in these dynamics. Not only do I bring my own Imagined Group with me (as explicated in this book, for example!) and one which I need to constantly bring to my awareness in order to be able to focus on this group with these members. I will also be the object of imaginings around what a good facilitator "should" and "must" do. I am thinking here of the participants who come to me after a session and tell me what I "should" have done when this or that happened.

Vignette 11, Denmark

In this latter case, I am also reminded of a recent two-day workshop for Gestalt therapists. On opening day two, I asked for reflections, reactions, responses, questions etc., from Day 1. A participant expressed the opinion that it had been an interesting and evocative day, and that he was still looking forward to seeing me "work". It transpired that, for him and, indeed, three others (4 of 12), my work as a Gestalt group practitioner involved me doing a series of individual therapy sessions in the group. The Imagined Group here was a collection of discrete individuals and the group facilitator essentially an individual therapist working with individuals though in plenum.

A methodological point here: yes, there are any number of more or less predictable Imagined Groups in the world, including this one of Gestalt therapists aged 50 – 70. And yes, as a member of that age-group myself, I am well aware that this generations' training experience would in all probability have been that of relentless individual work in a group setting. Such experience is fully embodied rather than rational only. Telling such a group in advance that they may have expectations of how I work that will not necessarily be the case is only providing a cognitive distraction.

I will always prefer to wait until the theme emerges – as above – and then work with it, often simply by raising awareness of its possible presence, using a concrete example from the interactions of the group dynamics.

The Emergent Group

Theoretically, the Emergent Group is AS IF the Actual Group is working its way into and maybe through itself as the Imagined Group, and becoming in its integration of that process the Emergent Group that only it uniquely can become.

The Emergent Group emerges dynamically in the self-organising and self-regulating of the existential field of group members in their actual and imagined interactions and the increasing complexity of their group dynamics. The change process over time offers glimpses of the Emergent Group in each temporary and usually brief state of equilibrium, often expressed by what I characterise as a "restful silence".

The Emergent Group is always in process, through its dynamics. It is present both in the dynamics of the moment at the same time as it is present in the process of its becoming and changing over time. It is at one and the same time, the end of the past of the group, the here-and-now of the dynamics of group-in-process and also the seeds of its emerging future.

It is the current expression of the evolutionary process over time of this particular collection of people, as they deal with simply being together in time and space, and maybe even simultaneously also performing individual or shared tasks as a work group or even team.

The Emergent Group is the phenomenal other of the facilitator's life-space. It is such both as an entity and also as the individuals and sub-groups which are figural for the facilitator at any given moment in the dynamics of their interactions.

The Emergent Group is ephemeral, of the moment, here...gone, newly here, gone again. It is what keeps us as facilitators, managers and leaders on our toes. We need to be present, aware and responsive - and accept our vulnerability in never being absolutely sure where a group is going, only where it may have been and right now is in our experience of being with it and in its dynamic presence.

The Emergent Group is the here-and-nowness of this Actual and Imagined Group, always emerging, always being and becoming simultaneously. It is AS IF the Emergent Group is the evolutionary potential of this Actual Group as it deals with being itself and also this Imagined Group.

There's a sense in which the Emergent Group is an example of a spontaneous collective mutuality of

Buber's "I – Thou" moment, the moment in which we transcend our separateness (Being Apart from) and become one (with each and all A Part Of The Whole). Certainly a transpersonal experience, and, for some, a spiritual moment in which a possible manifestation of the divine in Buber's terms is present. I have been with a small number of groups when this moment occurred, out of nowhere, in a restful silence which emerged as individual voices shortened their inputs in lowered tones and what was also a collection of individuals became a fully present social-psychological entity. And then an Actual Group again, with traces of the Imagined Group...

To even for a fleeting moment consider such an event as inevitable or desirable is to invalidate the intrinsic creativity of Buber's I-Thou moment. This happens, by, in and of itself – or not. And if it happens in a group you are facilitating, just sit back and enjoy being a natural part of it all, which is what you are. It did NOT happen because of anything particularly clever that you did to them. Your presence was enough. It simply happened with them and you are there – so enjoy!

Lewinian field theorists use the construct need to refer to the core organising force of any field, that which moves inexorably towards its own actualisation. A paradox here is that the organising need is usually not obvious until the organising process is completed. In other words, we know where any Emergent Group has been heading when it gets there. The Emergent Group is always the best possible version of itself at any moment in its emergence and, naturally, when it gets to where it has been going.

Using yet another extrapolation from physics much loved by field theorists, the Emergent Group is the attractor of the field of this Actual and this Imagined Group. It is what this collection of people becomes as they self-define, individually and collectively, as a group.

Allow me here to state the obvious: a Team is a Work Group so available to the dynamics of its interpersonal relatedness (Social Group) AS WELL AS its inter-functional role relations (Work Group) that the process of the Emergent Group of the whole is supported and evolves organically.

Implications for Practice

This is an aspect of my work which excites, enthrals and intrigues me.

Let me use a metaphor or two as I try to clarify: it is AS IF the Actual Group, those I call Adam, Birgitta, Charles, Denise, Eric etc., had already started weaving a carpet or maybe even a tapestry, called The Imagined Group...a carpet to stand on or a tapestry to look at and admire.

Then they meet, these people in this space, now, maybe with a shared past and also for a foreseeable future. It is then that the Emergent Group makes its appearance in a parallel loom to the one where the Imagined Group is being woven. The distinct patterns now being woven on this parallel loom are the characteristics of this unique Emergent Group. Patterns may be borrowed, adapted, unraveled from the Imagined Group loom, though now inextricably woven into this new carpet/tapestry. My task is to notice and acknowledge the patterns as they appear. I am not the designer – the group is. I am not the weaver – the group is. I am, along with the rest of the perceived group environment, part of the background against which the emerging patterns are figural foreground.

This is now the Emergent Group, my environmental other in the dynamics and process of the group's emerging and of our relationship, whether I am a group facilitator, manager or leader.

In other words, the Emergent Group is not some fully developed ideal group (whatever that is). The Emergent Group is that which is here-and-now and also becoming in the dynamics of the moment. It is the potential inherent in the change process over time. It is the current state of the evolution of this group.

So: no phases, stages or sequences or cycles of development towards some hypothetical and definable optimal state. In its emergence, a group is always the optimal version of what it can be in the moment, and always what it needs to be as it organizes itself in its change process over time. Construed as a living organism, a group evolves in its interactions with its physical environment. Construed as a social-psychological entity, it evolves in its interactions with its environment, whatever that may be: a facilitator, manager, leader, organization, market, society.

Any group is neither more nor less than a collection of human beings in a socio-cultural setting, dealing individually, interactively and ultimately collectively with the existential dilemma of being a part of/apart from other group members. This includes dealing with any number of variations on this theme appearing in the dynamics and process of its resolution of this dilemma. There is no solution to this dilemma. There is however a continual creative resolution of the tensions it evokes in and through the dynamics of group members, and the particular change process over time of this particular group.

The ensuing patterns of interaction will always be unique to this collection of people.

The Emergent Group is an expression of the change process over time, the evolution of this collection of people into whatever they can become, at any given moment. Every moment in a group's life is at one and the same time an in-the-moment cross-section of that process in its becoming as well as a culmination of the process to date. The Emergent Group is always as whole as it can be for the moment, always a perfect gestalt of where the Actual Group is in its evolutionary change process.

And always, always, uniquely so.

Meeting, respecting, exploring and supporting this uniqueness – and my part in and of it - is my only task as group facilitator or consultant. I need to repeat this: I honestly see my task as facilitator or consultant to a group, to first and foremost learn to get to know it as it is in any moment as a Social Group.

As manager of a work group, I will also need to attend to the performance of the functional tasks involved, and find the supportive balance that allows my staff to be both persons and functional roles. As consultant to a work group, I will need to explore where it is in the moment as a Social Group and how this influences it as a Work Group, whether of individual or connected functional roles.

Leaders do this intuitively, which is how they became leaders – they acquired followers who trust the leader's good intentions and respect.

The good news and the bad news is identical: there is nothing the practitioner does to a group that turns it into one thing or another, or a better or worse something. That is to objectify a collection of people. This is, of course, possible and even necessary where a

Work Group is involved, where the functional roles are concerned. There is Adam the person and Adam the accountant: as a manager, my expectations of Adam as a person are reasonably unique to him and me in our interpersonal relationship; as an accountant, there is a different set of quantifiable expectations I can have and – for Adam as a salaried employee – even a set of reasonable demands I can make in the context of our inter-functional connections.

From a Social Group perspective, the practitioner works with a group as its social-psychological environment, supporting its natural evolution through being a respectful presence as the most immediate social environment of the group and its members.

And all of this is within the parameters of the socio-cultural boundaries and their porosity or otherwise. This is the particular challenge for the expatriate manager or travelling consultant: to perform competently within two sets of boundaries, those of her own background culture and behaviours, and those of the local environment in which she is a visitor and also a guest, welcome or otherwise, as well as in a performing functional role.

There is a wonderful vignette in this regard of an expatriate U.S. subsidiary manager in Greece, determined to "empower" his subordinates as he had been trained to do. Ultimately, this led to such confusion and, indeed, disempowerment amongst staff more accustomed to orders that many senior people threatened to resign. And, of course, by threatening to resign they may very well have been "empowering" themselves, Greek style!

For sources of such cross-cultural management examples, please refer to the Recommended Reading list on page 106.

Part 3

A Focus on Practice

Introduction

Having presented my theoretical thinking and its expression in methodology with practical examples, I am now turning more explicitly to groupwork practice and presenting how my thinking informs that practice.

Core to this is a description of how I run an open personal and professional development group. By "open", I mean available to the public, and generally time-limited inasmuch as there will be a designated starting and ending date. Many such groups start this way, and end up leading to a more long-term engagement if a core sub-group chooses to negotiate for a new contract. Whatever, this starts as a basic open group and situationally neutral. By this I mean that it is not say, a group of bankers, or teachers, or employees of the same organization, though may contain such formal sub-group clusters. Such an open group is representative only of itself. It is, at one and the same time, an Actual Group embodying and ready to express its Imagined Group, in silence, words or deeds. As it meets for the first time, it becomes an Emergent Group. It is a Social Group and Work Group where individual professional development is concerned. If a core group or sub-group emerges which collectively contracts with me as a facilitator, then this may well be a team. I have had a recent experience of such a change process: a group of 11 members who had individually contracted with me to do a professional development training, 3 X 3 days, residential. At the end of that, a sub-group of 9 members contracted collectively with me to do a further 3X 3 days residential. And then a sub-group of 8 for a 3 X 3 day residential, and then another. Currently, this core group of 8 members has arranged to meet 3 times a year, both self-led and with contracted facilitators. Various combinations of them are now working together as freelance trainer partnerships. This group is now, I believe, a team and, as such, has contracted with me to facilitate a specific transitional journey in its understanding of its change process. I am offering this description of a group as the simplest example of how I work, without the specifics of organizational or commercial demands. Having presented my work with an open group, I will then look at a number of organizational settings where the approach presented can be applied. I am not proposing a prescriptive or normative approach. This is simply a description of how I operationalise my thinking, expressed above, in practice. I believe in what I do and in how I do it.

Facilitating an Open Group

Let me begin with a summary of my basic approach to groups from the perspectives previously presented. Since this approach, both theoretically and methodologically informs my practice, I want to be explicit about it – again.

- The group is that particular collection of three or more members who have registered to join and who attend regularly – what I call the "Actual Group".

- Members also bring with them their past experience of groups, their knowledge, assumptions, wishes, expectations etc. I name this the "Imagined Group", which can be seen as the bridge from the there-and-then of previous groups to the here-and-now of this "Actual Group".

- The "Actual Group", taken as a whole, is different to the sum of its members as a collective – I call this the "Emergent Group".

- The work of the "Emergent Group" – continuously becoming a group - is done by the members who are present at any given time.

- Group members are thus involved in both the in-the-moment dynamics of the Actual Group and the change process over time of the Emergent Group as an expression of the evolution of the Actual Group.

- In other words, the Here-and-Now dynamics of the parts are embedded in a Then-Now-Next process of the whole.

- I have no desired or required outcome, nor normative model, for the evolutionary group process of change, which I see as a self-organising and self-regulating social field.

- As the formally designated facilitator, I am not a member of the group.

- At the same time, together with its members, I and the group are of the field of the facilitator-members-our environment.

- Individual members very quickly become subsumed into sub-groups, explicitly in words and deeds or implicitly in thought-filled silences.

Whilst all of the above points are more fully explained, justified, debated and described earlier, this list will, I hope, suffice as a summary input to my practice as I now continue.

Some Terminology

I will here introduce some terms I use in my group work, both for my own orientation, and for that of group members:

- PROCEDURES

- PROCESS

• DYNAMICS

• INTERVENTIONS

PROCEDURES are any formalized and recurring events which are likely to occur, and which carry enough predictability of occurrence to be included as part of the practical planning. For example:

"Today's/Tomorrow's Logistics",

"Open House Sessions",

"Reflections and Applications",

"End of Module Feedback"

"End of Programme Feedback"

"Logistics": Questions around starting and ending the formally scheduled group-work time each day, length and frequency of breaks, length of lunch and dinner breaks, variations due to special circumstances such as dietary requirements, accessibility etc., are all put out as a shared responsibility to be treated with great flexibility.

It is quite usual in my experience for issues around time to become more and more an aspect of the group's dynamics and thus its process, than any logistical or procedural point. However, no matter what happens, I will bring them up at the beginning of a course and of each module; also at the end of a module in respect to the following module.

I use "Open House" sessions at the beginning of every session or module (except for the first one – see below), usually each morning, and sometimes also after a lunch break. It is a fully open session where members can say whatever they choose, need, wish to say; they are free to respond to one another, ask questions, and add perspectives. I remain fully present throughout, my active participation being in my awareness of what is happening for me, and what patterns of behaviour or theme may come to my awareness as the session develops. This for me is where group members find how they can/cannot and want/don't want to relate to one another.

Please note that an Open House session is anything but a "round" in the sense of every voice being heard – including that most enforced paradox of them all: saying that you have nothing to say! An Open House is just that: everybody welcome in their own time, at their own pace, and an excellent opportunity for group members to begin their experience of how a group not only self-organises but also self-regulates as each person responds to the experience of their membership.

I will generally respond to any comments directed at me. Where questions are concerned, I will often ask that I be allowed to respond more formally in a "teaching" session on theory and/or methodology. My intention here is to allow space for experiential learning and to position myself as facilitator/leader rather than group manager, in a directive or controlling sense.

I always include formal and scheduled sessions for reflections and thoughts around application, both personally and professionally. These are briefly reported in plenum in order to share learning in the group as a whole.

"End of Module Feedback" is just that – a 30 minute or so session (depending on numbers and the dynamics of the module) before we close the module devoted to comments on anything and everything pertaining to the experience of the module, one another, and I.

PROCESS and DYNAMICS are as described earlier in this book.

INTERVENTIONS are any action (including inaction) by me in my role as facilitator vis a vis the group, sub-groups and/or its members. Naturally, interventions by group members also occur and they are not within the frame of my formal responsibility while indubitably of the field of our togetherness.

Let me now try to put these together in a context.

Starting a Group

Whether I have used a traditional mail-shot, or spread my group information by e-mail, the central message is that the group members themselves and their interactions are the core personal and professional developmental agents. As facilitator, I present my two main functions as I see them. The first is to support the group with appropriate experiments and interventions intended to follow and raise awareness around the group's own process and the contributions of its members. The second is to use interactive teaching sessions based on actual and current events in the group as an aid to the members' understanding of individual, interpersonal, sub-group and collective aspects of group life, thus supporting an experiential/cognitive whole for each group member.

Already here with this opening paragraph to this section, it is clear that different therapists/facilitators will want to present their core message and their function differently as they market their competence and their group work. I like to be general enough to leave myself room to manoeuvre when I sit there with the group for the first time and begin the co-created contracting process – for the first though probably not the last time (see below). I like to keep my written course descriptions as simple, clean and clear as possible, and leave the complexities to the opening session when the working contract is negotiated for the first time.

Giving a maximum number of members is important, as well as a minimum number to start the group. My usual minimum for an open group is 7, for a closed group 5. I tend to set a limit at 12, though can go to 14 at times. The starting time/day and ending time/day for each module are clearly and unambiguously stated, as are costs and what they include. It is also useful giving information on how to register and pay, and a confirmation that every registration will be quickly acknowledged.

I generally prefer to give my e-mail address for any questions that may arise, rather than my phone-number, as e-mail gives me time for a considered response. There is also the fact that I have had my fill of calls at 7.30 a.m. or on a Friday evening as I settle down for the weekend - so e-mail! Where individuals specifically request that I phone them, I will do so.

And then we meet, all of us, face to face as a defined constellation for the first time, here and now together…

A Note about Numbers

Various schools of group work and authors have posited ideas about group size. In summary, five to eight members is regarded as a small group, with a preference for eight. From there to fifteen would be a medium-sized group. In my own opinion, above fifteen we are definitely looking more at a small organisation than a group. My own take on this issue is to do with the probability that, at some stage in the question of numbers, sub-groups will become more indicative of group dynamics and process than individual members (see below). I believe this begins to be the dominant dynamic with a group of three. Each additional member adds layers of complexity. I find ten-twelve manageable, and above that moves us all into a level of complexity which some members will find overpowering and therefore disempowering. I regularly work with training groups of twenty where I need to accept that I will never have a clear and detailed picture of what's going on, and work fully at the level of the group-as-a-whole, including sub-group dynamics.

A Sample Module 1/First Session Opening

I still tussle with the timing of my presentation of myself – first or last? Clearly, if it is a group that has gathered as a result of advertising then I will need to be welcoming, and more so if it is taking place in my house, as is often the case with residential sessions. Increasingly, I have tended to welcome the members, and say that I will wait to say a few words about myself and then the work we may be doing until after they have each presented themselves to us others. This is a matter of context and preferred style, and I encourage new facilitators to experiment freely, respectful both of their own style, the context and the group members.

Those times I present last allow me to match my content to that of the members and make connections with them where appropriate, such as having had the same trainers, or shared interests, or any connection which was figural for me as the members presented. (One of my favourites was a professional academic, socially un-practiced, totally new to the thought of doing personal work in a group, who switched from speaking of his nervousness to speaking enthusiastically about the Steve Earle (American singer-songwriter) concert he had attended earlier that week – as had I. His face visibly lit up when I mentioned this as I presented myself. A therapist who also likes Steve Earle!).

I will then move towards logistical matters, such as the availability or otherwise of tea/coffee making facilities, the whereabouts of toilets, smoking areas and so on. If on a residential, then logistics will include some choices around timing and length of lunch-breaks, whether to have evening sessions (much loved by some) after dinner, or a later dinner and thus a longer afternoon session. Or starting times in the morning. Such issues allow people with special requirements, such as diabetics for example, or people on a strict diet, to have an opportunity to legitimately give voice to their needs. Talking logistics is also a content-based topic which allows the members an opportunity for their first exchanges around shared issues, an opportunity to take each other's measure, to get a first feel for THIS group, THESE people. The work has truly started!

I will then turn to the program, course or whatever commitment they have registered and paid for. Clearly, if it is a training group with an institute, then there is probably a module description which I have certainly seen, maybe even written, and will need to have as figure in the context of the training. The same will roughly apply to a group on a specific and advertised theme. For therapy or personal/professional development groups, the work is more open-ended, the content less predictable.

Whatever the focus, I find that I can support all the variations within the framework of Procedures, Process and Dynamics – and now I add INTERVENTIONS. So, for example, I will present my take on the possible work we will be doing in some version or other of the following: the work of this group is primarily experiential and thus centres around its process over time – from morning to afternoon, day to day, module to module – and the specific dynamics which occur in the moment, however apparently or un-apparently related to the process they may seem. My interventions as therapist and/or facilitator will be focused on…and here the full context and my own preferences play a major part.

The options as I see them are:

1) one-on-one work with individuals;

2) and/or supporting interpersonal issues between members as they arise;

3) and/or intervening primarily if not exclusively with the group members as-a-whole, which will include sub-groups rather than an individual or one to one interpersonal focus.

In some groups, my role covers all three points. In others, I will declare a focus on point 3), and suggest that they themselves take care of the individual and the interpersonal work as natural aspects of group life and dynamics. My focus on point 3) is particularly relevant where Gestalt group-work training groups are concerned, as well as with management training groups, since group-work and group leadership are an aspect of the experiential learning involved.

The other aspects of my interventions will include interactive teaching sessions, as much as possible figural to actual events in the group as ground. The content here will clearly include generic material, and I find that timing is of the essence here. Introducing a didactic history of group dynamics session in the middle of charged, dynamic events is probably not the best timing in the world. Or it may be just that! Nothing is given with groups, apart from the fact that nothing is given…

I will here also present to participants the procedures of our sessions and modules, as described above. A summary on a flip-chart of this kind of opening would look something like this:

•An experiential focus on the group's own process and dynamics.

•Facilitator interventions at the level/levels agreed.

•Facilitator theory input sessions, based on and/or exemplified by both of the above, or at the request of a member/members.

•Recurring procedures as described, as a support structure.

Having thus taken my responsibility as convenor and/or assigned facilitator, I then throw this framework open to the group for questions, discussion, change or confirmation. This is negotiating the working contract, now that the business contract of registration and payment etc. is either behind us or in good progress towards completion. It is very important during this contracting that I stay with and hold myself at the aspect of content and not process. During this contracting session, I am not their contracted therapist, for example, and they are not my clients. This in fact, is one of the issues we are negotiating. Any behaviour on my part which disrespects this disrespects the group members.

It is not unusual for such items as "individual work" and "confidentiality", for example, to be brought up here. Depending on the context and the agreed theme, I will or will not agree immediately to work individually with individuals. I may even end up agreeing to do it with some specified people, and not with others; or work individually on request.

As for confidentiality – who can make a "rule" of such a minefield? For my part, I explain that I am ethically and legally bound by my profession as therapist to maintain confidentiality. Where such exceptions are applicable, I will explain that I am legally bound to report child abuse, and danger to self and others through a threat of suicide, violence or murder. Otherwise, I will certainly bring my work with the group to my supervision and not in any way identify or make possible the identification of any particular person. Should any episodes of our journey together find its way into one of my articles – which is always likely – then the people concerned may even have difficulty recognising themselves. Otherwise, the issue of confidentiality is up to them to resolve as they need to, following an open discussion.

This is yet another content issue which gives a taste of future dynamics and process as the group members work their way through their individual needs, doubts, indifferences, demands, requests, "oughts" and "shoulds" in this discussion.

I also like to leave the door open here for any other issue any member wishes to raise that can be addressed at this point, and allow it to run its course. This can include such items as "rules" about attendance, absence, late arrivals, early departures etc, etc. In such cases, I am willing to state my own preferences, invite others to do likewise, and let the exchanges continue until some form of consensus has been reached – or not! In this way, group members get a sense of their own responsibility, both individually and collectively, and also of their influence on me and each other.

My focus throughout this opening session is to establish a working contract which will inform our work together. All contracting specifically to do with my role is always open to re-negotiation at the opening of any session or module, when I will anyway always remind group members of our previously agreed working framework. Both then and otherwise, I will also reserve the right to explore the possibility of this re-negotiation as an expression of group process and/or dynamics.

As I trust is clear, my work as group facilitator starts from the moment I advertise or arrive at the location of the group. The opening session, including the logistical and contracting aspects, is very much intrinsic to the wholeness of the work. It is not unusual for some group members to regard these scene-setting sessions as time-wasting, and wonder when the "real work" will begin. They usually define this as the formal session, led by me, and including exercises and/or therapy and/or teaching. This is my opportunity to clarify that, from the moment we committed to this group, we had started working together. Our every interaction, from then and now on, is part of our work, including scheduled sessions with a fixed starting and stopping time, coffee breaks, lunches, strolls in the grounds whether alone or with others, evening gatherings in whatever constellations, contacts between sessions and so on, and so on. This may now become yet more material for our discussion in the here-and-now of the opening session.

And Then What?

At some stage, the initial contracting comes to a close, however provisionally. This may be at the end of the first of a series of weekly meetings, or the first opening sessions of a residential.

After the punctuation provided by a break of some sort – coffee, end of weekly session, whatever – I move to the next step. Until the initial contracting is completed, my role has been that of convenor or chairperson. Now, I am in my formal and contracted role as facilitator. I like to then move to introducing the "Open House". This means inviting group members to give us their voices, their silences – to give us who and where they are in the moment, and to respond to each other as they feel appropriate. This is now where our contracting goes from words to actions.

From this moment on, I am in the wondrously unpredictable any-man's land of group process and dynamics. Whatever happens is of the field of us, here in the room. We bring our past selves and our relationship to them, our present co-creating selves and our relationship to them, and our potential future selves in their becoming and our relationship to them. We bring that of our environment which impacts on us, for example, a training institute, a war, an impactful news-item, a family issue. We bring our selves into the room, influencing and being influenced, and always open to change.

People speak and are met with silence, affirmation or an invitation to dialogue. This is how sub-groups emerge, in group members' reactions to each other – "she's right, he's stupid, I hadn't thought of that so she's worth listening to, he seems to know what he's talking about, I knew the moment I saw her that I wouldn't like her and I was right", and so on...and so forth...

A Note on Sub-Groups

A sub-group is any constellation which implicitly or explicitly shares an attitude or opinion which becomes expressed through behaviour in the group. Sub-groups may be formal or informal; they can also be stable or dynamic (and everything in between!).

Formal sub-groups are generally explicit: male, female, gay, straight, lesbian, bisexual, trans, older, younger, married, single, parents, non-parents, black, white, of one nationality or another, employees, self-employed etc. Some of these are immediately obvious, others may have become apparent during the presentations, some evolve as people to get to know each other.

Informal sub-groups are those which form in the moment and which may or not last beyond that moment. Members who agree or disagree – vocally or in silence – with a statement by another member have joined a sub-group supporting that opinion, whether they know or intended it. Many of these silent and invisible sub-groups form more more concretely during breaks, walks, evening gatherings and other non-scheduled group time. They bring their energy into the room as a force of our field, a vector, one of the many self-organising and self-regulating forces of the group process and dynamics.

Amongst these will be my fan-club sub-group as well as that of my critics and that of the un-influenced either way. Each of these is a huge magnet, an attractor, as support, as challenge, as question-mark. Every teacher knows the temptation to "preach to the converted" and keep the fan-club happy – or deal with the critics, whether through confrontation or appeasement or whatever. I work hard at bracketing the various attractions of these particular sub-groups, and seeing them as expressions of the whole group's dynamics and process. After all, I may very well be the most figural environmental other for the group, individually and collectively, and the dynamics involved in relating to me are part of our work together. For me, the interpersonal has now moved from the traditional level of individual and other individual, to the more complex level of sub-group and sub-group, each representing a force of the field of our togetherness in our setting.

As such, sub-groups can represent such forces as sameness or change, process or structure, being or doing, closeness or distance and so on. The work of the Emerging Group is now being done by the sub-groups of the Actual Group, in the moment and therefore also over time. The practical aspects for the facilitator in working with sub-groups are dealt with below.

A Note on Informal Leaders

I am the formal leader, either as initiator or through being assigned as such by a senior management of some sort. My status includes particular responsibilities, authority of some nature whether as perceived by members or as delegated by management, an assumed competence, and more. While much of my status has strong cultural connotations, there is anyway and always a hierarchical relationship of some nature between the formal leader and group members. Whatever else applies, removing a formal leader is a major event and effort for a group.

Informal leaders are of two types: the self-appointed and the group-appointed. The self-appointed informal leader does not necessarily have any followers in the group, though this can change according to circumstances. The group-appointed informal leaders (plural!) are created by sub-group followership, and may not themselves be aware of their position. They are people whose comments, actions and participation evoke support amongst others inasmuch as they (the informal leaders) in some way represent the others, however temporarily. And this is a crucial distinction: an informal leader can be "deposed" effortlessly, simply by their vocal or silent followers switching allegiances.

As such, it is seldom crystal-clear for me when a member's work is to be responded to as "individual". Apart from always being field-emergent anyway, I will tend to explore to what extent the presented issue is at least just as much a sub-group issue as anything else. The implications for our practice are covered below.

And Then What? Continued...

With the first "Open House" up and running, the dynamics of the group emerge in terms of work. Some patterns and themes from the opening session may well make a re-appearance. Variations and new themes will also emerge.

My work here is to raise awareness of these dynamics as they emerge for me as figures and bring to the attention of all, in support of whatever change processes may be at work. For example, take "process" and "structure". Some members may be expressing a preference for more facilitator-led exercises (even giving examples from other groups); others may be expressing their appreciation of open, more process-oriented sessions. This is where sub-grouping and informal leadership can become apparent, as the theme becomes figural. I will share my awareness of the theme as I experience it – in this case structure/process, giving the data of my phenomenological observations as ground for the figure of the theme. So the comments I heard, the nods I saw, the silence of others – all the data I have gathered and now selectively shared, which group members can now use to inform their responses. Whatever then happens, sub-groups will become temporarily somewhat more defined.

I will then invite them to participate in what may be something of a paradox: an experiment with overtones of an exercise, fully process oriented! Should there be agreement, I will ask the people whose comments introduced the theme, to repeat them. I will ask anyone who more or less agrees to join the speakers. I add that anyone is free to move to another grouping at any time.

Each grouping is invited to share their perspectives with each other. This is followed by an invitation to each grouping to explain their perspective to the others. Depending on the atmosphere in the room – serious, playful, confused and withdrawn – I may suggest to each grouping that they do their best to "sell" their perspective to the others.

In this way, the group has an opportunity to explore a common theme which emerged as figures from the group as ground, voiced by some members and now "gestalted" in the here-and-now by all. As the movements settle, accelerate, settle again and the group arrives at a sense of where it is collectively, work is occurring spontaneously both individually and interpersonally. Awareness becomes insight and potential change. The experiment closes as I invite group members to re-configure in self-selected groups of minimum three, maximum five, to share their experience and their learning – and their questions, confusions, curiosities. I then offer the opportunity to share these in plenum – in effect, a theme-focused "Open House", which then becomes the ground for further figures.

I have become attached to "minimum three, maximum five" for self-selected small group work. This format offers everyone a choice where "being in the limelight" is concerned – somewhat more possible in three than five. It also gives everyone an opportunity to have their voices heard, to the extent they choose. In addition, this is a natural part of the sub-group and informal leader dynamics and process. Finally, time-management is easier: a twenty-thirty minute frame covers most eventualities.

It is never my purpose that everyone will have said everything they want to say. Whatever is spoken or left unspoken is still anyway ground for the continued work in and of the group. This methodology – sharing my awareness of emerging figures which, if meaningful to the group, are worked with experientially and experimentally – then becomes a general feature of the group work as we continue on our way into the specific world of this group as it unfolds over time.

A Note on Teaching

Adding a cognitive element to an experiential group, while often decided by the setting is also a natural ingredient here. The choice is often between "before or after". In other words, how much knowledge input will support a group in advance of experiential work, or is such work the necessary foundation for cognitive learning? In some cases, where the process work seems to be temporarily at rest, I may punctuate the work with a general input which is neither building on that which has gone before, nor preparing intentionally for what may follow.

I always find it most exciting to be able to use some current or recent dynamics or process issues as a stepping-stone to some theoretical input. An example here might be a piece about phenomenology when members comment on the differences between their experience "of the group" and mine, when I have suggested an emerging figure. This is a good example of making a cognitive connection to our experience.

Change over Time

As mentioned earlier, some themes – however group-specific they may be in the details involved – can be recognised as, in some way, typical of other groups also. This is the basis for the many group models which exist, and the exercises which often accompany them. These models are often generally linear and sequential, often normative in consequence if not intention. Most of us have a particular favourite and tend to apply it. From a Gestalt perspective, staying with where the group is in the moment and trusting that whatever movement in any direction which is appropriate will be taken, is the basic stance. It is precisely in this process and its relevant dynamics that learning can take place. All learning brings change, just as all change brings learning.

In other words, our skill as group practitioners lies in our willingness and ability to track and follow the group's process, rather than prescribe and direct it in any direction. The group really does know best about its own potential, about that which it may become.

I have no desired outcome for any group. My pride will sometimes push at me to show how good I am by "giving" them a great group experience – whatever that is. I'm still learning to recognise the signals of this push, and attending closely to how much of it is traditionally mine all mine, and how much is me-with-the-group. Is this a group desire resonating in me? How cleanly can I share this as material for the group to work on? This is where competence and experience transform into co-created art as we explore such a core issue with as much mutual transparency as we can manage.

At the same time I need here to deal with my sense and experience that a collection of individuals somehow becomes a group, easily distinguishable from any other group. This is what I have, above, called the Emergent Group, that distinctive "something" (or even "someone"!) which is different to the sum of its individual members. Co-creating this is what I have called the process of the group over time, from one apparent state of relative stability/constancy to another. This moving is through the in-the-moment dynamics of the members as they both co-create and grapple with the disequilibrium involved in the shift.

From the perspective of practice, I find that I am becoming more relaxed and even more accurate at using my awareness of the co-created me/group contact-boundary where process and dynamics are concerned. When I am feeling relaxed and confident in the presence of the group, with a sense of "where it is", then it is probable that the process has slowed into a period of relative stability/constancy. I will usually draw the group's attention to this, and ask for any comments.

When I am feeling lost, confused, isolated, pulled in different directions – then it is likely that the dynamics of change are in the room. While I have no guarantees that I am "right", I am prepared to trust my feelings and experience as the only reality I have. One of the dilemmas here is that group members are likely to be so into what's going on, that any sharing of my feelings is usually met with blank faces and question marks blinking like Christmas decorations around the room. So I attend more closely to the contact-boundary dynamics that seem to be thematic amongst the members.

An example here might be: "I notice that some of you are making comments and suggestions and I hear no responses. Sometimes, I have heard a change of topic which I found difficult to follow. Does this make any sense to any of you?" If my observation has any value to the members, at least one of those whose inputs have had no impact is likely to reply in the affirmative – or not! Whatever, the group now has an observation to relate to about their possible interpersonal and sub-group dynamics. Awareness may have been raised for some and may well become a topic of conversation during the next break. Whatever, the theme of taking in/keeping out the influence of others is now at least of the field, ground from which a figure may soon emerge. I see the contact-boundary dynamics of taking in/keeping out the influence of others as one of the many ways in which sub-groups can form and informal leaders emerge.

In other words, I work with attending to both process and dynamics, with the dynamics always being in-the-moment, and the process a sign of evolutionary change over time.

Closing the Door and Locking-Up

With the exception of on-going and open-ended groups, most groups have a scheduled first and last meeting - in other words a defined beginning, middle and end. Part of my responsibility as facilitator is to orchestrate the beginning and the end, by providing sufficient structure to support each of these formal elements. The first of these is easier (see above), since we are all concerned with similar issues at more or less the same place and time, entering something new together. The second is more delicate and more complex. As we approach the transition from the middle to the beginning of the end, group members can literally be "all over the place", though in the same room at the same time. Some members and sub-groups can't wait for the end to finally come; some become aware of missed opportunities which they may want to revive; some project their own unfinished issues onto others, encouraging them to take their last chance; some…well, if you have ever been in or facilitated a group, you will know how endless this list can be.

At some stage – the third-last session of a weekly group, the opening session of the final module of a formal programme, or other appropriate point in another setting – I will present the structure of how we will be ending. This will typically include a clear indication of the final "Open House" session which will end with a punctuated long coffee break, or lunch on a residential. This is followed by an extended "Reflection and Applications" session, covering the whole programme, with a plenary session where the combined learning of the group emerges in all of its disparate glories.

"Finished and Unfinished Business" – this is where each member has an opportunity to address each of the others with whom they feel that they have had issues of one sort or another, and either finished to their satisfaction or still feel are alive and well and will not be finished in this group. Then, a final "Feedback Session", this time for whole course, followed by the first and only traditional round, including me, to formally close and end our work, and say goodbye to each other.

Applying this Approach in an Organizational Setting

Vignette 12, Australia

What follows is a description of a organisational consultancy where I used the approach presented here in this book. This chapter was first drafted the day after the consultancy had taken place. An added ingredient is that the work happened to be witnessed, and the witness – let me call him Gerard - has had an opportunity to comment on the draft. Gerard is a fellow Irishman, friend and Gestalt colleague, who, like me, has lived outside of Ireland for most of his life. When I visit Gerard and his family, they will usually arrange some work for me locally, either with training groups or organisations. On this current trip, Gerard was going to give me his feedback on the latest draft of the book you are reading, and so was particularly well-versed with my thinking.

Gerard had arranged some workshops for me in a number of non-statutory organisations and also an informal, open session with the staff of a Women's Refuge. This was not a formally contracted consultancy with an agreed task or remit – rather an opportunity for the staff to meet an external, visiting "expert" in one thing or another around groups and organisations, and to engage with him (me!) in an open-ended discussion of whatever issues came up. This is precisely the working context I most appreciate, and know that it is not for the faint-hearted amongst managers and professionals. I also know, from experience, that my appreciation can easily blind me to the fact that it may well be only the manager who has this open willingness, or only some, though not all of the staff. So I know the need to curb my enthusiasm and wait and see what actually happens.

Gerard and I were greeted by Amy, one of the counselling staff, and I then met four other women, including Bea, the founder of the Refuge. A fifth woman, Carol, was unable to attend that day.

Gerard introduced me, something of my background, and something of the work I had done with staff in the organization where he is a senior manager. He then handed over to the staff and quietly contained his presence. I then learned that Bea had been working with the Refuge from its beginning some 26 years ago – and the newest member, Dorothy, for about 5 months. Dorothy is a mature student doing a Social Work degree and on placement with the Refuge as part of her degree. Another part was observing the work of the Refuge and preparing a brief report with commentary.

At any one time, the Refuge could house four to six sets of mothers and children, depending on numbers. The women were getting themselves and their children out of emotionally, psychologically, sexually or physically violent relationships and in need of safety, respite and support as they made yet another transition in their lives: the majority of the women were immigrants and – if not Russian – then coloured, the latter often Thai or Filipino. The local language – English – was generally a second language for these mothers and their children.

As Amy, Bea, Dorothy, Edith and Frances spoke and the themes flowed freely around the table I found myself sorting and selecting between themes. Clearly there was good evidence of those themes that would involve me doing "my" thing – for example, social groups, work groups and teams and the obvious team skills available to this manager and staff. So I bracketed such thoughts to leave space and freedom to meet the emerging figure of their interaction with each other and with me, and me with them. My comments are usually few and far between until an energized figure emerges and attracts my attention as a potential meeting-place between us, a place where contact and change can occur.

This is the art of field attunement, of being so fully of the social field of me/environment that energy-shifts leave a trace, an influence, and sometimes an attraction to respond and interact.

Such a shift occurred for me in the space of two successive interactions. Bea was talking about how staff and guests meet as equals around the table, and in their various activities and in working together on the issues that arise. The others nodded, smiled and made mumbled agreements. Almost instantly, Edith, who had previously said little, stated how important it was for the staff to act as role-models for the women. Again, nodding, smiles and mumbled agreements.

I could feel and sense a dissonance here in many aspects of who I am – cognitively, emotionally and empathically. I could not reconcile everyone "being equal" with everybody else as staff and clients, while some staff were also self-defining as being "a role model" sub-group for the client sub-group.

One of the skills of a field attuned practitioner is to be fully present and selectively share awareness – of self, of other, of self-other. And so I tried my first explicit intervention – that is interrupting the current flow between the staff and inserting my reaction into - and then seeing what happens.

So I said something to the effect that I had heard two statements in quick succession, both of which seemed to be greeted with agreement from the others, and yet, together, they formed a contradiction of sorts for me. I quoted Bea as accurately as I could, and then Edith. Bea instantly began explaining the special nature of how women function and work with each other. I agreed that this was something I had observed and, as a man, not ever really been naturally able to participate in – and that how women function and work together was not my focus. My focus was on raising awareness around two statements from staff members, one of which explicitly assumed equality and one of which explicitly assumed at least a behavioural differential of some sort.

At this point, Dorothy joined in with some thoughts about "power differentials" from her Social Work studies.

I suddenly felt a need to share a related experience with the Refuge staff, one that often comes back to me when I am trying to validate good intentions while putting them into a context which shifts their meaning: I am working with two colleagues, a black Ghanaian male and a white South African female on a Diversity Workshop outside Capetown, South Africa. One of the participants is a black South African psychologist. Let me call him Adam. Adam and I seemed to connect easily and well, and we both had a liking for banter. During a coffee break, I was in the main room talking to my colleagues, opposite opened double-doors leading into the foyer where the breaks were held. Adam crossed the opening. I waved casually to him. He immediately put down his cup and plate and walked quickly towards me. "Yes, Seán" he said, "what can I do for you". "Nothing" I said. "I was only waving to you". "Oh" he said – "I thought you were beckoning". In a moment of stunned, mutual insight, Adam and I looked into each other's eyes. We nodded. We embraced. "Adam, do you think we can use this for the workshop?" I asked. "We must, Seán, we must" Adam replied.

It was one of my most shattering experiences of the dynamic relationship between intention and perception. Here I was, a white, left-wing liberal giving a friendly wave to a black man, Adam. For Adam, I was 50 years of oppression, of being beckoned to, summoned. However lyrically I could express my intention of being equal, Adam had an experience of power differentials that were likely to linger, just as my anti-Britishness does.

There was a palpable silence. Dorothy then added that in their classes on diversity they had explored the difference between tolerating difference and accepting it as equally valid, also.

In retrospect, I am aware here of what I call a "choice-point", a will I, won't I moment. I could sense words forming sentences in my mind. At moments like this, it is as if the field of our social engagement with each other, the themes and energies of our interactions, are looking for a voice. My choice here is always whether to be that voice or allow the theme to find a more appropriate choice. There is a huge difference in the impact between "The Irish Oracle said..." and "maybe we could look at..". Wisdom from within a group, team or an organization often leads to painless organic insight and change. So I chose to remain silent and see what ensued.

Shortly afterwards two of the client women came in with a large plate stacked with home-made spring-rolls, and a lovely dish of stir-fried prawn and vegetable noodles, for the staff and their guests, Gerard and me.

As the staff, Gerard and I had our lunch, we closed the session around the table with the staff confirming that they had had some insights around issues that they would be able to deal with in coming staff meetings and retreats.

The Gestalt field perspective and methodology allows for the emergent creation of shared meaning as the dynamics and process of a group – even over a couple of hours – weave their unique patterns.

From my perspective as presented in this book, at least two sets of dynamics and processes were evident in this comparatively short piece of work. One had to do with the staff as a Social Group and also a Work Group and potentially a Team; one had to do with the Actual Group (that of staff, and also that of staff/clients), and then two Imagined Groups – "all equal" and "role models"/others. As the Actual Group of the staff members processed these Imagined Groups with which they mostly seemed to identify to some extent or another, then a potential team Babushka seemed to be emerging.

At the willing risk of being over-pedantic, this is a good example of how meaning and evolutionary change emerge from within the team as an organism adapting to an environment – me, as facilitator/consultant – feeding back my experience of the organism's dynamics as an intervention, and allowing the organism to find its own meaning.

In Conclusion.

I have intentionally kept this book short and as practically focused as I could. I have attempted to use theory to inform methodology and practice. As such, this was not a "HOW TO" manual. It was rather an encouragement to think maybe differently from usual, and see how this impacts on your perspective, your meaning-making, and, of course, your practice.

My hope is that you as practitioner can extrapolate freely from the gestalt of this book, taking the theory, methodology and practice I have presented and transforming it into your own practice, informed also by your own take on theory and methodology.

So this book is a foundation rather than a finished building, a seed rather than a flower or bush in full bloom.

So: over to you!

CPSIA information can be obtained
at www.ICGtesting.com
Printed in the USA
LVOW04s1831080416
482783LV00013B/209/P